AF708475

The Builder's Guide to Contracts and Liability

Second Edition

Legal Department
Builder and Association Services
National Association of Home Builders

Home Builder Press
National Association of Home Builders
15th and M Streets, N.W.
Washington, D.C. 20005

The Builder's Guide to Contracts and Liability
Second Edition
ISBN 0-86718-340-3

(c) 1989 by the National Association of Home Builders of the United States

All rights reserved. No part of this book may be reproduced or utilized in any form or by any means, electronic or mechanical, including photocopying and recording or by any information storage and retrieval system without permission in writing from the publisher.

Library of Congress Cataloging-in-Publication Data

The Builder's guide to contracts and liability.

ISBN 0-86718-340-3
1. Construction contracts—United States—Outlines, syllabi, etc. 2. Breach of contract—United States—Outlines, syllabi, etc. I. National Association of Home Builders (U.S.) Builder and Association Services Division. Legal Dept.
KF902.Z9B85 1989 343.73'07869 89-13717
347.3037869

For further information, please contact:

Home Builder Press
National Association of Home Builders
15th and M Streets, N.W.
Washington, D.C. 20005
(800) 368-5242

Publisher: Home Builder Press
National Association of Home Builders
Editor: Doris M. Tennyson
Art Director: David Rhodes

1/90 Uptown/Reproductions 3K
2/91 Reprint 3.5K

Acknowledgements

David C. Smith, NAHB president in January 1986, appointed a Builder Liability Task Force in response to NAHB members' concerns about their liability and insurance problems. The Task Force was charged with studying the liability and insurance issues facing the builder. The first edition of *The Builder's Guide to Contracts and Liability* was one of the major results of the work of the Task Force. This second edition of the *Guide* again provides builders and others in the construction industry guidance for writing good contracts and implementing effective customer service, two keys to controlling or limiting liability. The Task Force members included Leonard Miller, chairman, of Pembrook Pines, Florida; James Irvine of Portland, Oregon; Sandford Miot of Miami, Florida; Ivan Wohlworth of Massapequa, New York; Marty Azola of Brooklandville, Maryland; John McKay of Wichita, Kansas; Jack Shine of Encino, California; Ken Mitchell of Raleigh, North Carolina, Pat Casey of Oklahoma City; Frank Newton of Charlotte, North Carolina; and Harold Palmer of Austin, Texas.

This second edition was prepared by William H. Ethier, litigation counsel, NAHB Legal Department, and Michele McDaniel, former associate litigation counsel.

Figure 6-1, "Sample Home Maintenance Instruction Checklist," and Figure 6-2, "Sample Punchlist," were revised by Dick Morris, NAHB construction technology and codes specialist.

Contents

Introduction 5
Warning 5
1. Construction and Sales Checklist 7
2. Contract Between Builder and Buyer or Owner 11
2-1. Caption 11
2-2. The Contract Documents 12
2-3. Description of Work To Be Performed 12
2-4. Price, Deposit, and Payment 12
2-4A. Price and Deposit 12
2-4B. Costs to be Reimbursed 13
2-4C. Application for Payment 14
2-5. Financing and Other Contingencies 14
2-6. Delays and Early Completion 14
2-6A. Liquidated Damages and Unavoidable Delay 14
2-6B. Bonus for Early Completion 15
2-7. Differing Site Conditions 15
2-8. Changes in Work 15
2-9. Termination of the Contract 16
2-10. Notices 16
2-11. Arbitration 17
2-12. Time of Commencement and Substantial Completion 18
2-13. Inspection, Acceptance, and Possession 18
2-14. Ownership of Plans and Specifications 18
2-15. Conformance with Plans and Specifications 19
2-16. Representations and Warranty 19
2-17. Entire Agreement and Severability 20
2-18. Conveyance 20
2-19. Effective Date and Signatures 20
3. Environmental Liability in Real Estate Transactions 21
Hazardous Waste Liability 21
3-1. Inspection Provisions and Option To Terminate Contract 22
3-2. Cooperation from Seller 23
3-3. Seller Warranties 23
3-4. Indemnification from Seller 23
Radon Liability 23
3-5. Reducing the Legal Risks 24
3-6. Radon and Real Estate Transactions 24
3-7. Radon Contract Provisions 25
4. General Building Specifications 27
5. Warranties and Disclaimers 29
Express and Implied Warranties 29
Limited Warranty 30
6. Inspections 39
Home Maintenance Instruction 39
Presettlement Walk-Through and the Punchlist 39
7. Certificate of Acceptance 47
8. Contract Between Builder and Subcontractor 49
8-1. Subcontractor Proposal 49
8-2. Payment Terms 50
Option 1—Contingent Payment 50
Option 2—Savings 50
8-3. The Scope of the Work 50
8-4. Changes 50
8-5. Insurance and Indemnification 51
8-6. Taxes, Charges, and Permits 51
8-7. Cleanup 51
8-8. Liquidated Damages 51

Figures

Introduction

I-1. Ten Ways To Prevent Liability Problems 5

1. Construction and Sales Checklist

1-1. Sample Construction and Sales Checklist 8

3. Environmental Liability in Real Estate Transactions

3-1. Potentially Responsible Parties 21
3-2. Steps for Recognizing a Contaminated Site 22
3-3. Steps for Reducing Builders' Radon Liability Risks 25

4. General Building Specifications

4-1. Items Usually Included in Specifications 27

5. Warranties and Disclaimers

5-1. Federal Trade Regulation Requirement for Warranty Documents 30
5-2. Federal Trade Commission Advisory Opinion to the National Association of Home Builders 31
5-3. Sample Limited Warranty Agreement That Excludes Items Covered by the Magnuson Moss Act 33
5-4. Sample Limited Warranty Agreement Conforming to the Magnuson-Moss Act 35
5-5. Sample Statement of Nonwarrantable Conditions 37

6. Inspections

6-1. Sample Home Maintenance Instruction Checklist 41
6-2. Sample Punchlist 44

7. Certificate of Acceptance

7-1. Sample Certificate of Acceptance 48

8. Contract Between Builder and Subcontractor

8-1. Sample Proposal 50

Introduction

Over the past few years the members of the National Association of Home Builders have become more and more concerned about the many lawsuits filed and the increasingly large judgments assessed against home builders and others in the construction industry. The procedures and forms in this *Guide* were written in response to these concerns of NAHB members.

Builders' potential liability can be reduced in a number of ways throughout the construction process and in the ensuing sale of a home. Builders should implement sound risk management practices in every phase of their businesses to limit their liability. Well-written contracts can eliminate or reduce many of a builder's risks. Conscientious customer relations and quick followup on punchlists and call backs also will prevent many problems from developing.

A list of actions that can reduce liability problems appears in Figure I-1. Builders should keep these items in mind at all times.

The goal in producing this guide is to help builders and general contractors control or limit liability in the construction and sale process. Other parties in the construction industry, including subcontractors, suppliers and remodelers, can also benefit from much of the advice in this guide.

This second edition of *The Builders Guide to Contracts and Liability* contains a substantially revised Chapter 2, "Contract Between Builder and Buyer or Owner. The contract provisions in Chapter 2 are now better organized. The suggested contract language throughout the *Guide* has been made more concise, and a completely new Chapter 3, "Potential Environmental Liability in Real Estate Transactions," has been added.

Figure I-1. Ten Ways To Prevent Liability Problems

- Use a well-written contract for all transactions in the construction and sales process. Both parties to the contract should read and understand all provisions before signing the document.
- Examine your insurance program and make sure it is comprehensive. Fill in any gaps in insurance coverage.
- Do not create unrealistic construction schedules.
- Follow all building codes and other regulations to the letter. Do not cut corners.
- Use reputable subcontractors and establish sound working relationships with all parties in the construction process.
- Do not make promises you cannot keep to potential buyers during the sales process nor during construction. Screen brochures, advertising, and other marketing devices for unintended promises or warranties.
- Keep customers happy and follow up quickly on punch lists and call backs. Avoid polarization of the parties to the contract.
- Use indemnity clauses in contracts with subcontractors and design professionals.
- Disclaim implied warranties or obtain waivers of such warranties in states where they are permissible.
- If all else fails, avoid going to court. Use alternative dispute resolution techniques, such as arbitration or mediation.

Warning

The forms and procedures contained in this package are simply illustrations. They should not be used without the approval of an attorney experienced in construction contract law.

The suggested contract provisions do not and cannot apply to every situation. Applicable law differs widely among the states, and in many cases, local municipal law requires special treatment. Some of the provisions may not even apply to a particular construction project, and they may weaken a builder's position with respect to that contract. This information is intended only to identify certain issues and highlight some alternative possibilities. It is offered as a service to builders to help them identify certain potential problems that need to be considered carefully and discussed with an attorney.

In the "Sample Language" the words in brackets [ ] are not part' of the contract provision, they suggest to the reader a way or ways the provision could be modified.

Builders should have their attorneys prepare documents that meet their particular needs.

1

Construction and Sales Checklist

The sample construction and sales checklist (Figure 1-1) provides a format for working with the home buyer throughout the course of a construction project and the sale of a home. The checklist is intended to remind the builder of the tasks that ordinarily should be performed to satisfy legal and professional requirements. The checklist should be started at the beginning of the builder's relationship with the buyer and used as a permanent record for the buyer's and the builder's actions and decisions.

This checklist is designed merely to suggest an approach to recording approvals by the buyer and activities accomplished. Before using it, builders should tailor it to fit the needs of their individual businesses and construction projects. Most of the items will apply only (a) when builders are constructing homes on lots already owned by the home buyers or (b) to custom homebuilding situations. Other items apply solely to the more common situation in which builders own the lots on which they are building. Still others apply to both situations. Some actions or methods necessary for a particular builder or product may not be included in the checklist.

Space has been provided at the left side of the checklist items to record the date and (where applicable) for the builder and the buyer to initial the items. The right side of the checklist contains space for comments by the builder. The checklist is cross-referenced to the other parts of this *Guide.*

One of the major advantages of keeping such a checklist is to assist the builder in the event of litigation. Cases often reach the evidence gathering stage long after a project is completed, and the parties have difficulty recalling or substantiating their recollection of what actually happened. A clear record kept in the form of a checklist, log, or diary will assist builders in restructuring events and demonstrating, not only what they did, but also that they kept the buyer informed.

The existence of such a record may help to deter groundless litigation.

Figure 1-1. Sample Construction and Sales Checklist

Dates	Builder's Initials	Buyer's Initials	Item	Comments
______	______	______	Determine buyer's financial capabilities/method of payment.	______
______	______	______	Prebid conference.	______
______	______	______	Submit bid.	______
______	______	______	Submit initial construction documents to buyer.	______
______	______	______	Obtain performance bond (if required by law).	______
______	______	______	Obtain labor and material payment bond (if required by law).	______
______	______	______	Deliver bonds to buyer (if required by law).	______
______	______	______	Deliver certificate of insurance to buyer.	______
______	______	______	Secure and pay all necessary payments.	______
______	______	______	Notify buyer of list of subcontractors (see Chapter 8, "Agreement Between Builder and Subcontractor").	______
______	______	______	Provide buyer with estimated progress schedule.	______
______	______	______	Obtain copies of all property insurance policies from lot owner/buyer.	______
______	______	______	Determine whether hazard insurance is necessary.	______
______	______	______	Discuss warranties on personal property with buyer. Make specific warranties available for buyer's examination (see Chapter 5, "Warranties and Disclaimers").	______
______	______	______	Obtain construction (or sales) contract (see Chapter 2, "Contract Between Builder and Buyer or Owner").	______
______	______	______	Review contract with attorney before executing it.	______
______	______	______	Present builder's limited warranty and list of nonwarrantable Items to buyer.	______
______	______	______	Explain and have buyer execute documents. (see Chapter 5).	______
______	______	______	Execute contract with buyer. (see Chapter 2).	______
______	______	______	Obtain utility (water, gas, electric) permits in lot owner's/buyer's name.	______
______	______	______	Submit regular (weekly, monthly) statements to buyer for payment.	______
______	______	______	Consult with buyer regarding changes in plans or specifications. Obtain written change orders.	______

Figure 1-1. Sample Construction and Sales Checklist (cont.)

Dates	Builder's Initials	Buyer's Initials	Item	Comments
________	________	________	Keep dated records of discussions with buyer regarding progress of work, e.g., "field meetings."	________
________	________	________	Walk through house with buyer and fill out punchlist. Assist buyer in identifying all items that need improvement and establish timetable for completion (see "Presettlement Walk-Through and the Punchlist" and Figure 6-2).	________
________	________	________	Complete punchlist items (see Figure 6-2).	________
________	________	________	Walk through house with buyer and fill out the "Sample Home Maintenance Checklist" (Figure 6-1).	________
________	________	________	Have buyer initial completed punchlist items previously listed as needing improvement. Fill out new punchlist as necessary until all items are satisfactorily completed (see Figure 6-2)	________
________	________	________	Execute certificate of acceptance with buyer, Chapter 7, "Certificate of Acceptance").	________
________	________	________	Establish date for post-closing review of construction. Give buyer blank punchlist checklist to note necessary adjustments on warrantable items (see Figure 6-2).	________
________	________	________	Record all post-closing work.	________
________	________	________	Conduct post-closing inspection and obtain final punchlist approval from owner, (using Figure 6-2.)	________
________	________	________	One year after closing fill out followup punchlish and complete promptly (also use Figure 6-2).	________

2

Contract Between Builder and Buyer or Owner

A written contract records the exact terms of an agreement between parties. The agreement defines the scope and price of the product and, among other things, allocates the risks inherent in a particular transaction between the parties. This chapter of the *Guide* should help builders and their attorneys write construction contracts that lessen the builders' risk.

Many provisions in ready-made contract forms, such as the AIA Document A201, expose builders to considerable liability during the construction process. No boilerplate contract clause is suitable for every situation. Therefore, builders should critically examine every transaction into which they enter to foresee contingencies or events that could impair the transaction's benefits to them. They should make sure that each of their contracts is written to provide them with adequate protection from events that may expose them to liability.

In examining the various clauses that might be included in a construction contract, this chapter provides a "Comments" section that explains the purpose of a particular clause and "Sample Language" that may be used in construction or sales contracts between owners (or buyers) and builders. The comments for each provision help the reader to understand the sample language. These suggested provisions do not address every contingency, and they do not apply to all construction and sales agreements. Additionally, this manual does not cover all provisions that should be considered in a sales or construction contract. For example, parties should negotiate and document who will be responsible for such miscellaneous items as:

- Payment of hazard insurance and utility fees during construction
- Proration of tax and insurance costs upon sale of the property
- Bond requirements, if any
- Lien notices.

These and other provisions, if written correctly, may further protect builders against unnecessary liability.

Builders who offer an insured warranty to their customers should redraft or not use the warranty provisions contained in this *Guide* that conflict with their particular insured warranty program.

Contracts are legal documents that greatly determine a builder's liability if a home buyer alleges that the builder failed to perform the contract obligations. Therefore, an attorney experienced in construction contract law should prepare (or at least review) any such documents before a builder signs them.

Warning—The National Association of Home Builders has provided this guide and sample contract language merely to point out the types of provisions of which builders should be aware. These suggested provisions should not be used without review by an attorney.

This chapter addresses the major sources of potential liability that a builder may face in two different types of construction agreements:

- A construction agreement with a buyer who owns the lot or land on which the house will be located
- An agreement to construct a house on a lot owned by the builder and to sell the house and lot together.

Common sense will dictate which of the following provisions apply to a particular builder's needs.

2-1. Caption

Comments

The caption [2-1] should include the names of all of the home buyers (both husband and wife, for example, if they are buying jointly). The full legal name of each party should appear in all documents in the transaction. If a purchaser is a corporation or other business entity, the documents should include the full name and type of business entity. The names of the parties should be exactly the same in the contract as in all other project documents. The caption also should give a legal description of the property (e.g., lot, block, subdivision).

Sometimes buyers hire architects or construction managers who participate in the ongoing construction of

2-1. The caption is the heading or introductory part of a legal document.

the house. The contract should make the architect or manager the buyer's agent, and it should give the builder authority to rely on any representations, statements, revisions, and approvals made by the architect or manager related to the construction process. The contract also should specifically provide that the builder will not be held liable for any actions made in reliance on recommendations of the architect or construction manager.

If applicable, specify the name of the buyer's real estate agent.

Sample Language [2-2]

This contract specifies the terms between __(buyer's name)__, the buyer, and __(builder's name)__, the builder, to __(sell and/or construct)__ a home on the property located at: __(legal description of property)__. __[name of architect/construction manager]__ is the buyer's agent, and the builder may rely on any representations, statements, revisions, and approvals made by __[architect/construction manager]__, related to the performance of the terms of this contract. The builder will not be held liable for any actions made in reliance on recommendations of __[architect/construction manager]__,

2-2. The Contract Documents

Comments

The written contract specifies most of the terms of an agreement, but some terms are more fully described in other documents. For example, construction and site plans usually are not reprinted in full in the contract. Also, the builder's warranties and warranty limitations often are drafted separately (see Chapters 5, "Introduction to Warranties and Disclaimers," and 6, "Limited Warranty." If, however, the written contract specifically references these other documents, their requirements and limitations will be documented as part of the agreement. The contract should specifically and accurately describe the referenced documents by date, number of pages, plan number, name, and any other appropriate information. The requirements contained in the supplemental documents should not conflict with each other nor with the terms of the contract.

Sample Language

The terms of this contract include the conditions of this contract and, by reference, the provisions in the other documents specifically listed below. The terms of this contract govern over any conflicting provisions in the documents incorporated by reference.

The builder shall perform all of the work that is required by this contract and any documents incorporated by reference below.

Except for written modifications executed by both parties subsequent to the execution of this contract, the terms of the contract are limited to the provisions contained in this contract and the documents described as follows: __(title of document)__ dated the ______ day of ______ 19___, consisting of ____ pages; __(title of document)__, dated the ______ day of ______ 19___, consisting of ____ pages; __(title of document)__ dated the ______ day of ______ 19____ consisting of ____ pages.

2-3. Description of Work To Be Performed

Comments

This section should describe the project with particularity, as set out in the other contract documents. For example, it should include the location, approximate dimensions, and a legal description of the property as well as the names of the buyers.

The cost of the work and the builder's fee is based on the work described here. The scope of the work should be defined specifically enough to clarify whether changes by change order are within the general scope of the work contemplated by the contract. This section—

- Specifies what the builder will do
- Possibly describes the portions of the project for which each of the other parties is responsible
- Spells out the work to be performed and the builder's responsibility for subcontractors
- Authorizes the builder to purchase materials for the project
- Specifically identifies any unusual responsibilities that the buyer may request of the builder.

Sample Language

The project shall consist of and the builder shall perform all of the work that is required by the contract documents, as follows: ____________________
____
____
____
____

2-4. Price, Deposit, and Payment

2-4A. Price and Deposit

Comments

This section specifies and defines the builder's compensation for the construction of the structure. It also instructs the parties in the manner and time of payment. The contract should—

- Include the cost of the work. Some builders charge buyers a total fixed price for the project. Others bill on a cost-plus-fee or cost-plus-percentage basis. The contract should specify the type of fee schedule and outline all anticipated costs and fees, when applicable. In either case, the contract should specify the total price of the construction or sale transaction and the amount of earnest money deposit paid to the builder upon execution of the contract. The total price should be written out in both words and numbers. The contract should itemize the total price as—

- The deposit
- The buyer's mortgage(s) or deed(s) of trust
- The retainage or balance, if any, due at final settlement.

2-2. Sample language that appears in brackets presents an option for the reader. Depending on the particular transaction the reader must choose one or the other, both, or neither of the possible wordings presented.

• Identify the first and, if applicable, the second mortgage or deed of trust.

• Specify allowances for profit on change orders.

• Establish due dates for payment. Parties often arbitrarily set due dates for payment. The due dates should be mutually acceptable to builder and buyer and should reflect specific stages of construction. The contract must account for the time necessary for the builder to prepare an application for payment and for the buyer to make the payment.

• Require interest for late payments. For example, "Payments due under the contract but not paid shall incur daily interest at the rate of _______ percent (____%) from the date payment is due."

• Specify whether retainage is allowed. If the contract provides for retainage, the builder should insert a provision for holding the retainage in an interest-bearing escrow account and for disbursing it to the builder upon substantial completion of the project.

• Require evidence of financing. The builder should be allowed to verify that the buyer has satisfactory financing, including an allowance for subsequent change orders. The buyer can be made to produce evidence of financing before the builder is to commence work.

• Satisfy any special state or local requirements. Some states require that the contract specifically identify certain expenses (e.g., Washington state requires that the sales tax be listed separately from the total price).

Sample Language

Fixed Price Contract–The buyer agrees to buy and the builder agrees to construct [and/or sell] the building [and lot] for the consideration of $_______, _________ dollars (the total price). The buyers will pay $________ as an earnest money deposit upon signing this contract [or on or before some date other than the date the contract is signed] and will make a final payment in the amount of $_______ to the builder at final settlement [within ____ days of substantial completion].

Cost-Plus-Fee Contract—The buyer agrees to buy and the builder agrees to construct [and/or sell] the project for the consideration of the builder's actual costs and expenses, as defined in Section 2-4B, "Costs To Be Reimbursed," of this contract, plus ______ percent (___%) of these costs and expenses. The buyers will pay $_______ as an earnest money deposit upon signing this contract [or on or before some date other than the date the contract is signed] and will make a final payment (including all costs and expenses plus the fee specified above) to the builder at final settlement [or within ____ days of substantial completion].

2-4B. Costs To Be Reimbursed

Comments

This section is applicable to cost-plus-percentage or fee contracts. This list of items suggests some costs that may need to be reimbursed in a construction project, but it may not include all costs to be reimbursed on every job. Some of the costs noted here may be irrelevant for a particular project. The builder should include all relevant items and especially every contingency negotiated with the buyer. Builders should check this section against their general ledgers and other accounting practices to make sure all appropriate costs are included.

Many contracts will also include a section regarding costs not to be reimbursed. These provisions should be carefully reviewed because, by definition, they exclude some of the builder's actual costs. These items would be paid out of the percentage or fee added to the defined costs and, therefore, cut into a builder's profit.

Sample Language

The term *cost of work* means costs necessarily incurred in builder's proper performance of the work contained in the contract documents, including the following items:

• Wages, benefits, costs of contributions and assessments for Workers' Compensation, unemployment compensation, Social Security, taxes, or any other costs incurred by the builder for labor during performance of this contract.

• Salaries for builder's personnel to the extent their time is spent on work in furtherance of completion of this contract. This payment of salaries includes (but is not limited to) work performed at shops, on the construction site, or on the road for such items as expediting the production or transporting materials or equipment.

• The builder's and the builder's agents' reasonable travel and subsistence expenses incurred in furtherance of completion of this contract.

• Payments made by the builder to subcontractors for work performed pursuant to subcontracts under this agreement.

• Cost of land and all land development expenditures associated with or apportioned to this project.

• Cost of all materials, supplies, and equipment incorporated in the work and consumed in the performance of the work; cost less salvage value of such items used but not consumed that remain the property of the builder, including all costs of installing, repairing and replacing, removing, transporting, and delivering the machinery and equipment.

• Rental charges consistent with those prevailing in the area for machinery and equipment used at the construction site, whether rented from the builder or others, including all costs of installing, repairing and replacing, removing, transporting, and delivering the machinery and equipment.

• Sales, use, excise, or any other taxes related to the work imposed by governmental authorities.

• Impact fees, exactions, royalties, charges, inspection costs, or any other fees related to the work imposed by governmental authorities.

• Permit fees, royalties, or damages for infringement of patents and costs of defending related lawsuits, and deposits lost for causes other than the builder's negligence.

• Expenses for telephone service at the site, telephone calls, telegrams, postage, delivery fees, stationery, and other similar petty cash items related to work.

• Costs incurred for security at the job site.

• Costs incurred because of any emergency affecting the safety of persons or property.

• All landscaping and backfilling necessary under the contract documents, including the cost of all grading, removal or planting of trees, snow removal, frost breaking, water pumping, excavating and related work, the delivery to the site of the necessary materials, and the hauling away of excess fill and material or trash and debris.

• Builder's risk or other insurance, soil fees and civil engineering fees, performance bonds, and labor and materialmen's bonds in an amount equal to one hundred percent (100%) of the maximum costs.

- Differing site conditions, as provided for in Section 2-7.
- Any other costs incurred in the work that are within the scope of the work as defined in the contract documents, or any other overhead expenses.

2-4C. Application for Payment

Comments

The builder and the buyer may negotiate any form of payment schedule that is mutually agreeable. One alternative allows the builder to establish a draw schedule with the home buyer and construction lender. With a draw schedule, a specified amount (e.g., 10 percent) is paid up front, the builder can withdraw from the account at successive phases during construction, and the lender may hold a retainage until the structure is accepted by the buyer. A draw schedule should require the buyer to make or authorize each payment to the builder within a specified number of days after the builder's application for payment. Before requesting final payment, builders should ensure that all claims have been settled and should obtain signed confirmations from the buyer that, based on the final inspection, the contract requirements have been fulfilled.

The following sample language provides for an alternative method of payment.

Sample Language

The builder shall prepare [weekly, biweekly, or monthly] itemized statements for the buyer that specify all costs incurred by the builder in furtherance of performance of the terms of this contract.

Upon application by the builder for payment of costs incurred or to be incurred in the future, the buyer will place adequate funds in an account from which the builder may draw to pay for the cost of the work. Buyer will make funds available to the builder within ______ days of receipt of the statement, as provided for in the "Notice" provision of this contract.

The buyer shall make final payment to the builder, including the entire unpaid balance of the cost of the work and all other compensation due to the builder, as defined in Section 2-4A, "Price and Deposit," and 2-4B, "Costs To Be Reimbursed," of this contract at final settlement________ [or within _____ days after substantial completion of the work]

2-5. Financing and Other Contingencies

Comments

If the buyer needs financing, the builder should make the contract contingent upon a financing commitment from a lender. The contract should state whether the buyer or the builder (on behalf of the buyer) will apply for a mortgage. The contract also should specify the loan amount, duration of the amortization period, the maximum interest rate (including initial interest rate and potential increases if the buyer is contemplating an adjustable rate mortgage), and maximum points.

The contract should allocate payment of loan application fees and closing costs between the buyer and the builder. The generic term, *closing costs*, refers to many fees and expenses. To minimize disputes, the parties should identify and specify who will be responsible for the payment of each cost.

The buyer should agree to file a written loan application within a maximum of 7 days after execution of the contract and to file with at least three lending institutions, if necessary. The agreement should allow either party to rescind the agreement by written notice if the buyer does not receive a financing commitment within 30 to 90 days of the date of the construction or sales agreement. Finally, the contract should provide for the return of all deposits paid by a buyer who complied with the agreement's financing application requirements, but it should allow the builder to retain any out-of-pocket costs incurred in attempting to obtain financing on behalf of the buyer.

If, however, the buyer failed to diligently pursue financing, the contract should allow the builder to keep the deposit and to pursue any other legal and equitable remedies that may be appropriate.

A buyer who does not need financing should place funds equal to the total price of the agreement in an escrow account. Similarly, if the buyer needs only partial financing, the balance of the funds due should be placed in escrow.

Any other contingencies that the parties contemplate should be specifically identified. For example, if the agreement is contingent upon additional appraisals, inspections, or the sale of other property, the contract should specify the time period in which the contingency must occur, what will happen to the agreement if the condition is not fulfilled, and how the deposit money will be divided.

If the builder sells a lot to the buyer with the understanding that the builder will construct a house on the property, the lot sale should be contingent upon the buyer's execution of a construction contract with the builder within a specified period of time.

Sample Language

Builders should consult an attorney for specific language.

2-6. Delays and Early Completion

2-6A. Liquidated Damages and Unavoidable Delay

Comments

A liquidated damages clause requires a defaulting party to compensate the other person for expenses incurred as a consequence of the default. This provision specifies what constitutes a default under the contract and the amount of damages to be paid by a defaulting party. This type of provision may minimize damages in the event of a lawsuit brought on the basis of a default.

Contracts with subcontractors and suppliers should include a provision stating that they have read and are bound by the builder's agreement with the buyer (see Chapter 8, "Agreement Between Builder and Subcontractor"). This statement will put them on notice that the builder may be liable to the buyer in the event of a delay in construction, and if the delay is caused by a subcontractor or supplier, that firm may be liable to the builder for damages.

The liquidated damages clause should not impose a penalty on the builder, but it should reasonably approximate the actual losses the buyer will incur if the builder does not complete the building on time. Estimating actual losses a buyer would suffer can be difficult, and a liquidated damages clause may work against the interests of the builder. The purpose of the clause is to compensate buyers for expenses, such as hotel costs, until the home can be occupied. However, sometimes only minor problems can cause a delay that nevertheless can qualify as a breach for which the owner still may be entitled to liquidated damages and earn an unnecessary windfall. Careful drafting may minimize the potential for this inequity.

A court that determines the liquidated damages clause is, in fact, a penalty assessed against the builder may void the provision. The buyer then may assert the usual legal and equitable remedies. These may include all actual and consequential damages. Therefore, a provision should specify that the buyer's liquidated damages remedy is exclusive of all other remedies.

Sample Language

If the buyer must incur additional costs as a consequence of the builder's failure to perform the terms of this contract by its stated completion date (e.g., housing, moving, or travel expenses), then the builder will compensate the buyer in the amount of $______ for each calendar day of inexcusable delay until the work is substantially completed. If the builder's failure to perform the terms of this contract in full does not result in any additional expenses to the buyer, the builder's damages shall be limited to the cost of completion of performance of the terms of this contract. The buyer shall not recover any compensation from the builder for delay caused by differing site conditions, as defined and provided for in Section 2-7, "Differing Site Conditions," of this contract.

The builder will use its best efforts to complete construction of the project prior to the completion date. However, if reasons beyond the builder's control cause an unavoidable delay in the progress of construction (including, but not limited to, such factors as the unavailability of materials, inclement weather, strikes, changes in governmental regulation, acts of governmental agencies or their employees, acts of God, or the failure of the architect or the buyer to cooperate), the builder may, in its sole discretion, extend the date of completion for a period equal to the time of the delays.

This liquidated damages remedy is exclusive of all other legal and equitable remedies.

2-6B. Bonus for Early Completion

Comments

As a corollary to the liquidated damages clause, builders often include a bonus provision that entitles the builder to a per diem sum of money for finishing early.

Sample Language

If the builder substantially completes the work before the substantial completion date in Section ____ of this contract, the buyer will pay the builder the sum of dollars _______ ($_______) for each calendar day between the date when the work is substantially completed and the substantial completion date set by the contract.

2-7. Differing Site Conditions

Comments

Unexpected site conditions, such as a ledge, bedrock, or an unexpectedly high water table can be expensive to work around. This provision protects builders if these site conditions are encountered. It should include a clear definition of *differing site conditions,* and provide for notification, work changes, or contract modification procedures upon discovery of such a problem. An alternative to the clause provided below could require the buyer to pay the extra costs incurred, plus profit at a specified percentage of the cost. The builder also has the option of cancelling the contract. These suggestions would replace the equitable adjustment language below.

Under Federal Government contract law, the term, *equitable adjustment,* has an exact meaning. However, outside of this special area of law, the definition of equitable adjustment can be confusing. Builders' attorneys should check the case law precedents in their states to see how the term is treated by the courts, and it should be used only where the term has an identified meaning.

Sample Language

A differing site condition is a physical characteristic of the property that materially changes the construction techniques necessary to fulfill the terms of this contract. Examples of differing site conditions are subsurface or latent physical conditions at the site differing materially from those indicated in this contract, or unknown physical conditions of an unusual nature located on the building site.

Before disturbing any differing site condition, the builder shall notify the buyer of such a condition. The buyer shall investigate the condition within five (5) business days. If the buyer and the builder agree that the differing site conditions will cause an increase in the builder's cost of, or the time required for, performance of any part of the work under this contract, the issue will be resolved as follows:

A. If the total contract price will increase by more than ________ percent [e.g., 10 percent], the buyer may terminate the contract upon paying the builder for all costs expended to date and for the builder's full profits as provided in Section ______ of this contract; or,

B. The builder and the buyer shall execute a written specific cost adjustment to this contract, including any adjustments in the time for performance necessitated by the differing site conditions.

The buyer's failure to investigate the condition will confer authority upon the builder to complete construction of the project according to the terms in Section 2-6A, "Liquidated Damages and Unavoidable Delay," of this contract and the builder shall further be entitled to ______ [an equitable adjustment/payment of any increased costs necessitated by the differing site condition].

If the parties cannot agree on the existence or consequences of a differing site condition, the terms of this provision shall be arbitrated as provided for in Section 2-11, "Arbitration," of this contract.

2-8. Changes in Work

Comments

After the contract is signed and work commences, often the buyer will request that changes be made in the design or materials used. While working these changes into the project may be prudent, some construction contracts obligate a builder to continue the project even if a buyer disputes an obligation to pay for cost increases under a change order. These provisions do not entitle the builder to any payments for the change order work during the time it is being performed and may force the builder to wait until the project is complete before the dispute is to be resolved.

Before beginning any new work created by a buyer's request for a change, the builder should require that the buyer execute a change order. That change order agreement should be in writing, should specify the revisions in price and work, a revised payment schedule, if necessary, and a revised date of substantial completion, if necessary.

A dispute over how much the change order affects the contract price can cause delays in construction. Delays may be minimized if a provision in the contract requires the buyer to pay the builder for actual costs generated by the disputed work so that construction may continue pending resolution of the dispute. When the dispute is resolved, the buyer should be required to pay the builder for any pro rata profit on such work.

Sample Language

The builder is under no obligation to make any changes, additions, or alterations in the work requirements provided in the contract documents. Upon reasonable request of the buyer, the builder may make changes, additions, or alterations, but the builder shall not be required to do so until the parties have executed a written change order. All written change orders shall become part of this contract, and the buyer agrees to pay the builder for changes in the work on the same basis as specified in Section 2-4, "Price, Deposit, and Payment Provisions," of this contract.

If the buyer and the builder cannot agree on the cost of the change and the builder proceeds to make the changes, then the builder will receive from the buyer an equitable adjustment, including direct and indirect costs, plus __[5 or 10]__ percent of such costs. The buyer agrees to make requests concerning any changes, additions, or alterations in the work in writing directly to the builder named in this contract and not to the workers, including subcontractors, on the job.

2-9. Termination of the Contract

Comments

Occasionally, unpredictable or uncontrollable events substantially delay a construction project, and one party wants "out." The builder and the buyer can negotiate how to allocate responsibility for this possibility. The following clause illustrates only one solution. The parties may agree that if the buyer terminates the contract, the builder will keep any money earned up to the date of termination. Or the agreement may provide that the builder is entitled to a specified percentage of the builder's total anticipated profits. The contract also may require a buyer who terminates the contract without cause to pay the builder a sum of money greater than the amount of anticipated profits. This provision should not call the additional fee a penalty because a court will invalidate "punitive damages" clauses in a contract. However, a sum designed to compensate the builder for downtime while arranging for a new job or finding a new buyer may be justified.

The builder also may include a provision that allows the buyer to "cure" a termination within a specific time period by bringing all payments and other obligations current. This action permits the parties to reinstate the agreement so the builder can complete the job.

If the builder fails to substantially fulfill the contract terms, the agreement can allow a refund of the buyer's money. If the buyer owns the lot, the builder should subtract from the buyer's refund all out-of-pocket costs. The buyer and the builder also should allocate attorney fees incurred in connection with the termination of the contract. Another provision should address the event of bankruptcy of either party.

The contract should require that all termination notices be in writing (see Section 2-10, "Notices").

Sample Language

Builder's Remedies—If the buyer (a) fails to comply with the provisions of this contract; (b) terminates the contract for any reason other than the builder's failure to perform; or (c) orders the builder or the builder's agents, employees, or subcontractors to stop work to be performed by this contract, then builder may (a) terminate this contract and retain any downpayments and/or deposits as liquidated damages; (b) recover all unpaid costs, expenses, and fees earned to the time of default or termination, the prorated cost of overhead expenses, and the costs, fees, and prorated overhead expenses for all change orders approved by the buyer prior to the termination. (These costs shall be based upon the costs specified in Section _____ of this agreement.); and (c) institute judicial proceedings for specific performance and/or any other legal and equitable remedies.

Buyer's Remedies—If the builder fails to comply with the provision of this contract, then the buyer shall be entitled to a refund of all money paid to the builder. [If the buyer owns the lot, builder should refund money paid, minus out of pocket costs for the work performed, including a pro rata share of the builder's profits.]

2-10. Notices

Comments

The contract is written to minimize disputes about the terms of the agreement. Likewise, all notices provided for under the contract should be written. The builder should keep all records related to the project for at least the duration of the project. Ideally, the builder should store the records until all applicable statutes of limitations have expired. The statute of limitations is the period of time within which a buyer must file a law suit. That period of time can run for many years, and under certain circumstances, the courts may extend the limits indefinitely.

Sample Language

Any notice required or permitted to be delivered under this contract should be mailed to the parties at the following addresses:

(builder)	(buyer)
(street address)	(street address)
(city, state, zip)	(city, state, zip)

For purposes of this contract, notice is received when sent by certified mail, postage prepaid, return receipt requested via the United States Postal Service.

2-11. Arbitration

Comments

Arbitration provides a mechanism for resolving disputes without the publicity, and probably the cost, of litigation. Arbitrators, generally experts who may be more likely than a jury to understand the technical aspects of a construction controversy, may provide a more impartial forum for a dispute than a courtroom.

States vary in their willingness to enforce arbitration provisions, but the clear trend is to uphold an arbitration agreement. Additionally, the mere existence of an arbitration provision may deter potential lawsuits. Builders should suggest arbitration or mediation procedures early in a dispute, before a buyer begins to suffer "mental anguish" that a jury might find compensable in a damage award.

In a minority of jurisdictions, the results of arbitration will not prevent reconsideration of the case by a court, even when a contractual provision states that the arbitrator's decision is binding. Although the parties in these jurisdictions may attempt arbitration prior to filing a lawsuit, if one party decides to circumvent the process, a court may allow it. The arbitration proceeding can be supervised by a formal dispute resolution organization, such as the American Arbitration Association (AAA) or the National Academy of Conciliators (NAC). Typically, the AAA arbitrates commercial construction disputes and the NAC targets its services to home builders and buyers. Each has a formal set of procedural rules: the AAA uses its *Construction Industry Arbitration Rules*, the NAC uses its *Expedited Home Construction Arbitration Rules.*

An AAA proceeding under the *Construction Industry Arbitration Rules* can be expensive because the parties pay both the AAA and the arbitrator(s) of the dispute. Generally, the AAA assigns three arbitrators to a dispute.

Under the NAC Expedited Home Construction Arbitration Rules, one "dispute settler" with home construction experience is assigned to hear and determine the dispute. If requested, the NAC dispute settler attempts informal settlement (mediation) with the parties before rendering a final decision. This system tends to be faster and less expensive.

Alternatively, the parties can provide tailor-made arbitration rules either in the contract or in a separate contract document and thus eliminate the need for an arbitration association. For example, the parties can agree that each party independently will select an arbitrator and those arbitrators jointly will choose a third. Alternately, the parties may specify that only one arbitrator be involved (even when using either AAA or NAC). Using one arbitrator rather than three would substantially reduce the cost of the process.

The rules also should provide discovery and evidentiary rules, set time limits for presentation of each party's case, and limit the maximum damages allowed in the arbitrators' decision and award. Rather than start from scratch, the parties can agree to follow the dispute settlement procedures outlined in the federal Magnuson-Moss Warranty Act, 15 U.S.C.A. sec. 2301 et seq. (see also 16 C.F.R. sec. 107).

Builders should not mention alternative dispute resolution in their warranty provisions because they may be forced to use the Magnuson-Moss settlement procedures.

Sample Language

All disputes between the parties to this contract arising out of or related to any contract term(s), or any breach or alleged breach of this contract will be decided by arbitration unless the parties otherwise mutually agree in writing.

No arbitration proceeding under this provision shall include any person or entity not a party to this contract except by prior written consent. The written consent must specifically refer to this contract's arbitration provision, describe the matter to be arbitrated, and be signed by the builder, the buyer, and any other person or entity to be joined. An arbitration proceeding involving an additional person or entity is limited to the parties and matters described in the consent.

The arbitration shall be conducted by __(specify the organization or named arbitrator[s] agreed upon)__ in accordance with __[the rules adopted by the arbitration body chosen, the rules specified below, or the alternative dispute resolution proceeding specified in the federal Magnuson-Moss Warranty Act, 15 U.S.C.A. sec. 2301 et seq. [see also 16 C.F.R. sec. 107]. The parties reference the Magnuson-Moss Act only to provide rules of arbitration in the event of a dispute, and they specifically do not incorporate the Magnuson-Moss warranties into this contract.]__.

The parties must file a written notice of arbitration with the other party to this contract and with __(the arbitration association or arbitrator[s chosen__ with ______ days after the dispute has arisen. The notice of arbitration may not be filed after the date a claim based on the dispute would have been barred in a judicial proceeding by the applicable statute of limitations or repose.

Either party may specifically enforce (a) a decision rendered under this agreement to arbitrate or (b) any valid agreement to arbitrate with additional persons, under applicable arbitration laws. The award rendered by the arbitrator(s) will be final and binding, and any court with jurisdiction over the decision may enter a judgment upon the arbitrator's decision.

The two groups mentioned earlier can be contacted at the addresses listed below:

American Arbitration Association
1730 Rhode Island Avenue, N.W., Suite 509
Washington, D.C. 20036
(202) 296-8510

National Academy of Conciliators
7315 Wisconsin Avenue, 1255 North
Bethesda, MD 20814
(301) 907-7000

2-12. Time of Commencement and Substantial Completion

Comments

The date of commencement of the work should be no earlier than the date of execution of the contract. Instead of a specific date, a flexible starting date may be established by use of a notice to proceed, e.g., "the work shall commence on the date stipulated in the notice to proceed." The builder should have evidence of the buyer's financing before commencing work (see Section 2-4, "Price, Deposit, and Payment Provisions"). Before building on a lot owned by the buyer, the builder should require evidence of valid title and a copy of current survey, deed restrictions, and easements, if any. These items may help protect the builder's lien rights if a lien must be filed on the property for lack of payment, or they may identify potential problems with the site that the builder can avoid.

The date of substantial completion of the work may be a specific date expressed as a number of days (preferably calendar days). The contract should make clear to the buyer when "substantial completion" will occur (e.g., the date certificate of occupancy is issued, actual occupancy by the home buyer, or some other identifiable point of time). Also, if construction is connected to an interstate land sale, the builder must comply with time periods for delivery under the Interstate Land Sales Full Disclosure Act, 15 U.S.C. sec. 1701 et seq. (1982) (see 24 C.F.R. parts 1700-1730).

The contract should include a provision for extending the time of completion, as is done in Section 2-6A, "Liquidated Damages."

Sample Language

Assuming all conditions precedent are satisfied and weather permits, the work to be performed under this contract shall be commenced on _(date)_ and substantially completed no later than _(date)_.

2-13. Inspection, Acceptance, and Possession

Comments

Inspections allow buyers to identify, and give builders the opportunity to correct, defects in materials or workmanship. During the inspection period, the builder can document a buyer's satisfaction with the completed home. The builder should keep a record of the inspection for (at minimum) the duration of any statute of limitations or repose (see Figure 6-1, "Home Maintenance Instruction Checklist," and Figure 6-2, "Punchlist," in Chapter 6, "Inspections").

The contract should define *possession* and determine what steps the parties must make before the buyer takes possession. For example, builders often include provisions for inspection, formal acceptance, and final payment before a buyer can take possession. The sales contract should state that "time is of the essence," and require the builder and buyer to make full settlement of the terms of the contract by a specific date.

Sample Language

Prior to the closing, the buyer or the buyer's agent shall inspect the house in builder's or builder's representative's presence. At that time, buyer will give to builder a signed punchlist that identifies any deficiencies in workmanship or materials.

Builder shall correct any items on the buyer's punchlist that are, in the good faith judgment of the builder, deficient in workmanship and/or materials according to the standards of construction relevant to _(city, state)_. The builder shall correct those defects at its cost within a reasonable period of time _[not to exceed 30/45 days; as set forth in the limited warranty]_. The builder has no obligation to make any repairs not included on the buyer's signed punchlist, with the exception of those latent defects covered by builder's limited warranty set forth in _[Section __ or give title and date of limited warranty document]_. The builder's obligation to correct any defects shall not be grounds for postponing or delaying the closing or for imposing any conditions upon the closing not specified in this contract.

On substantial completion of construction, buyer shall execute the Certificate of Acceptance (attached and incorporated by reference into this contract). Buyer will not take possession of the project before inspection of the home, execution of the Certificate of Acceptance, and final payment to builder. This provision is subject to the right of either party to obtain an injunction or file for any other legal or equitable remedies.

2-14. Ownership of Plans and Specifications

Comments

If the buyer provided the plans, the builder should specifically impose liability for defects in the plans onto the buyer. Builders who provide the plans for a house, however, should expressly prohibit buyers from giving or selling those plans to other potential buyers or builders. The best way to ensure enforcement of this latter provision is to copyright the plans. Sample clauses are provided for both the buyer's plans and for the builder's plans.

Sample Language

Buyer's Plans—The builder agrees to construct the home in accordance with the building plans supplied by the buyer _(reference by title, author, and number of pages)_ Builder assumes no responsibility or liability for defects in the design or engineering of these plans. Buyer solely will be liable for any damages caused by defective or negligently drawn building plans, including but not limited to additional costs caused by delay in substantial completion of the home, additional costs for materials necessitated by any changes, additional labor costs, and pro rata profit on the additional work.

Builder's Plans—The builder has provided the building plans to be used under this contract _(reference by title, date, author, and number of pages)_. Buyer has no ownership rights in the architectural plans used under this contract, and the buyer will be liable to the builder in the amount of lost profits and all consequential damages for the reuse or resale of these plans.

The builder makes no representations or warranties about the quality of these plans except those specifically provided in the limited warranty references in this contract.

2-15. Conformance with Plans and Specifications

Comments

Builders must explain to their buyers that the actual construction of their homes may deviate somewhat from the plans and the specifications, or from models that the buyers may have seen. Furthermore, builders may want to protect themselves in the event of deviations from property lines, survey lines, and the like. These facts should be disclosed to the buyer in conversations at the beginning of the marketing and negotiation processes. In addition, these provisions should be included in the contract and in the Certificate of Acceptance, to be signed or initialed separately by the buyer as evidence that the builder disclosed the possibility of deviations or inconsistencies to the buyer. The buyer should initial each of the provisions in the "Sample Language" printed immediately below.

Sample Language

Construction of the House—The house shall be constructed to conform substantially with the plans and specifications that are set forth in the attached Exhibit(s) __(include numbers and names of exhibits)__ (the terms of which are incorporated in this contract by reference). The buyer acknowledges that in the course of construction of the house, certain changes, deviations, or omissions may be necessary because of the requirements of governmental authorities having jurisdiction of the property, suggestions and design changes made by the architect, or particular conditions of the job. The buyer hereby authorizes the builder to undertake, without the need for specific authorization, any changes, deviations, or omissions authorized by the architect, required by governmental authorities, or particular conditions of the job.___/___
(buyers' initials)

Building Dimensions—Building dimensions are approximate. The buyer acknowledges that in the course of construction of the house and the making of improvements on the land, certain changes, deviations, or omissions may result in a variation of the dimensions of the house. The buyer acknowledges and agrees that __he/she__ has not relied upon the accuracy of any representations made by the builder with respect to the square footage of the house. The buyer has not relied on any plans or specifications that are on file with any governmental regulatory authority.___/___
(buyers' initials)

Model Home—The buyer acknowledges that the builder has shown __him/her__ a model, or drawings, maps, or other documents depicting the house. The buyer understands that certain items and improvements to the house may vary (e.g., the decoration, the style, the type of appliance) and may differ from samples the builder may have shown to the buyer. The builder reserves the right to make changes and substitutions of materials of equal or greater quality than those shown in the model or specified on the plans and the specifications.___/___
(buyers' initials)

2-16. Representations and Warranty

Comments

The builder should discuss the limited warranty with the buyer at the beginning of the negotiations (see Chapter 5, "Warranties and Disclaimers," of this *Guide.*) Most courts will uphold limitations on or exclusions to the warranty if they are considered part of the contract. That is, when warranty limitations and exclusions are included in the give and take between the builder and the buyer when they are forming their agreement, the courts will usually enforce the limitations and exclusions.

But many courts also require that the disclaimer of implied or other warranties be conspicuously displayed in the contract to be enforceable. The disclaimer should be located either on the first page of the contract or just above the buyer's signature. Putting the disclaimer in bold type also may help. Finally, builders should require the buyers to initial this section separately.

Builders must clearly explain to their buyers that builders do not warrant any manufactured items or consumer products installed in the homes they build, not even if the contract requires installation of the products. Builders can assign the manufacturers' original purchase warranties directly to their buyers. Assigning warranties transfers directly to the buyers those warranties that the builders received when they purchased the goods for installation into the buyers' new homes. **Warning**—Some manufacturers do not allow assignment of warranties on their products, and the assignment of warranties is governed by state law.

If builders intend to warrant the manufactured items or consumer products installed in the homes they build, the warranty must conform to the "Magnuson-Moss Act" guidelines (see Chapter 5, "Warranties and Disclaimers," for a more complete discussion of this federal law).

The warranty limitations should also address environmental issues, such as indoor air quality, including radon (see Chapter 3, "Environmental Liability in Real Estate Transactions," for a full discussion of these and other environmental liability issues).

Builders must instruct all agents, representatives, and employees not to make any promises or representations to buyers without specific prior authorization from the builders. The builders' job site supervisors, managers, employees, and subcontractors who are likely to be in contact with the buyers should sign agreements with their individual builders acknowledging that they are not authorized to make representations, promises, warranties, and the like without prior authorization of the builders.

Sample Language

The limited warranty attached and incorporated by reference into this contract contains the sole warranty provided by the builder to the buyer. The limited warranty shall have no force and effect until the builder has received full payment of the purchase price stated above, and the warranty shall take effect at either the time of closing or the date of first possession by the buyer, whichever is first. The limited warranty excludes all items on the attached list of nonwarrantable conditions that is incorporated by reference into this contract.

The builder assigns to the buyer, to the extent they are assignable, all rights under manufacturers' warranties on appliances, equipment, fixtures, and consumer products included in the house and located on the buyer's property. The builder provides no warranties relating to manufactured or consumer products.

This contract contains all of the representations, warranties, and promises of the builder. No agent or representative of the builder is authorized to make any representation or promise on behalf of the builder other than those contained here, and the builder makes no other warranties, express or implied, including but not limited to the warranties of good workmanship, habitability, and fitness of purpose.

2-17. Entire Agreement and Severability

Comments

This provision emphasizes that this contract supersedes all previous agreements between the parties. It also assures that each section of the contract will be considered separately, so that if a court determines that one provision is unenforceable, the remainder of the contract will remain in effect. The merger clause, necessary only where the builder is selling the land or lot on which the house is built, specifies that the provisions of the contract will not become void upon transfer of the deed.

Finally, the parties can agree not to assign or sell their rights and responsibilities in the contract to another party. The assignment clause restricts the buyer's right to sell the contract (and its payment obligations) to another person who may not have adequate financial resources to pay the builder.

Sample Language

This contract and the documents incorporated by reference pursuant to this contract constitute the entire agreement between the parties, and may be changed only by a written contract amendment signed by all parties to this contract. The contract shall be binding upon each of the parties' respective heirs, executors, administrators, successors, and assigns. However, this contract shall not be assigned without the written consent of ___[the builder/all parties]___.

Each provision of this contract is separable from every other provision of the contract, and if any provision is unenforceable or revised, the remainder of the contract will remain valid and enforceable.

This contract will be governed by the law of the jurisdiction where the property is located.

The provisions of this contract shall survive the execution and delivery of the deed and shall not be merged therein.

2-18. Conveyance

Comments

This provision applies only to the sale of property. When a builder transfers property and, by necessity, the deed to the property, the builder will make certain warranties about the condition of the title to the property. The most common set of warranties are included in a general warranty deed. This type of deed assures the buyer that the seller has transferred clear title, with specific exemptions for commonly recorded information about the property such as covenants, easements of record, municipal and zoning ordinances, and any other liens or encumbrances specified in the agreement.

Alternatively, builders can supply either special warranty deeds, in which the sellers warrant that they did nothing to cloud the title. Or they can provide a quit-claim deed, which provides *no* warranties to the buyer. A quit-claim deed simply releases any ownership rights that the seller may have in the property. Builders should consult an attorney to determine the prevailing practice in their communities and for specific language.

2-19. Effective Date and Signatures

Comments

Ideally, all parties to the contract sign the document at the same time. If, however, that is not possible, this provision assures that the builder is not bound by the terms of the contract until the builder (or an authorized representative) has signed the contract.

If any changes are made to the contract after it is printed or typed, both the builder and the buyer(s) must initial each revision for it to be valid. Of course, any changes to the work after the contract is signed should be conducted pursuant to the change order requirements of Section 2-8, "Changes in Work," and any changes to the contract after it is signed require a written amendment according to Section 2-17, "Entire Agreement and Severability."

The buyer and builder should sign at least three original contract documents (Commonly available, multicolored carbonless, copy paper is useful for this purpose.) The parties should execute the contract in their proper capacities, as individual buyers or sellers, or as partners, officers, or directors of a partnership or corporation that is a party to the contract. The parties should use their complete legal names on all contract documents and any subsequent change orders or contract amendments. Once both parties have signed the document, they should complete and initial the date-of-contract provision.

Sample Language

This contract has no force or effect and will not be binding upon the builder until it is accepted and executed by the builder. This contract shall become effective on the date designated below or the day it is executed by both parties, whichever is later.

We, the undersigned, have read and understand and agree to each of the provisions of this contract and hereby acknowledge receipt of a copy of this contract.

______________________ (buyer's signature)	______________________ (name of builder)
______________________ (buyer's signature)	By______________________ (authorized signature)
Date ______________________	Title ______________________
	Date ______________________

This contract is dated, and becomes effective,

____
(month, day, year)

______________________ (buyer's initials)	______________________ (builder's initials)

3

Environmental Liability in Real Estate Transactions

Builders are exposed to several sources of potential liability for environmental hazards to the public or health risks to the buyer. This chapter discusses two issues that builders can deal with in their contracts when either buying property or selling homes to consumers: contaminated purchased property and indoor pollution.

Under the hazardous waste laws of the federal and numerous state governments, builders may be liable for damages and cleanup costs if they buy property that is contaminated with hazardous or toxic materials. A wide range of chemicals and products are covered by these federal and state laws. While not strictly an issue of liability to the home buyer, a builder's potential liability to these governments for hazardous waste cleanup is significant enough to warrant discussion in this *Guide*. Builders should recognize that in addition to hazardous waste liability to the governments (which are discussed below) consumers may file a law suit against the builder if a home becomes contaminated with hazardous waste or toxic materials.

However, these "toxic tort" cases are based on particular state tort laws (e.g., the laws of negligence, strict liability, and related legal theories). Therefore, they are beyond the scope of this *Guide*.

Indoor pollution, another major environmental issue of concern to builders, includes the potential liability to consumers for exposure to radon and other indoor air pollutants. While indoor air contains numerous potential pollutants, radon has taken a front seat in both the media and before environmental and health safety agencies. Because radon is the issue that consumers inquire about most often, this *Guide* includes a discussion of radon, how it affects (and should not affect) the real estate transaction, and how builders should treat the potential liability stemming from radon.

Other major environmental issues present potential liability for builders, but they are beyond the scope of this *Guide*, including—

- The builder's or developer's duty to comply with federal, state, and local laws concerning the preservation of wetlands or other environmentally critical areas
- Compliance with occupational, safety, and health regulations that are designed to protect employees and the community at large
- Compliance with a host of other laws regarding clean air, clean water, coastal zone management, and the handling and storage of toxic materials. Failure to comply with these laws can bring upon a builder or developer severe administrative and other penalties and damages.

Hazardous Waste Liability

This section explains potential liability for hazardous waste contamination on property owned by builders and developers (even if only temporarily). The sample contract language presented here may be included in land purchase agreements to limit potential liability.

The Comprehensive Environmental Response, Compensation, and Liability Act (CERCLA)—also commonly referred to as Superfund—authorizes the Federal Government to require four categories of potentially responsible parties (Figure 3-1) to pay for the release or threatened release of hazardous substances into the environment.

Any one of the parties in Figure 3-1 may be held liable for the entire cleanup cost regardless of negligence (or lack of negligence), amount of contribution to the contamination (if any), and compliance with laws in effect at the time of disposal.

CERCLA provides an "innocent purchaser" defense for

Figure 3-1. Potentially Responsible Parties

- The current owner or operator of the contaminated site
- Any person who operated a facility or owned a site when toxins were deposited
- Any person who created and disposed of the hazardous substances
- Any person who selected the site and deposited, treated or transported the waste.

property owners who can prove that they did not know and had no reason to know that any hazardous substance contaminated the property. To qualify for the defense, the party "must have undertaken, at the time of the acquisition, all appropriate inquiry into the previous ownership and uses . . . in an effort to minimize liability." CERCLA also provides a defense for contamination resulting solely from an act of God, an act of war, and acts or omissions by third parties not in a contractual relationship with the landowner. Persons who acquire property through inheritance or bequest are similarly exempt from liability.

Many states have enacted superfund-like statutes that impose liability on landowners for the cleanup of hazardous waste. The more burdensome regulatory and liability schemes require sellers to remove contamination before the property is transferred and that notice be given to purchasers or to the state prior to transfer.

Some states also have enacted "superliens" that enable the state to place a lien, superior to all others, to secure payment for the cleanup. In a few states, liens can be placed on all of the owner's real property in the state—whether or not it is polluted—to pay for the cost of cleaning up a contaminated parcel.

Hazardous waste liability is not limited to properties bordering industrial sites. Rural and suburban properties and groundwater are often contaminated by pesticides, seepage from underground storage tanks, and improper disposal of industrial or dry cleaning chemicals. Depending on the size of the lot or project, the prudent builder may want to hire a consultant to conduct an environmental assessment or audit of the site. The steps listed in Figure 3-2 will help (a) to minimize the risk of purchasing contaminated property and (b) to limit a builder's liability in the event the property is contaminated.

A real estate purchase agreement should allow sufficient time for the buyer to inspect the land for hazardous waste through an environmental audit. The audit generally reviews past practices, business records, and government documents. If warranted, actual physical inspection, testing, and sampling also ought to be performed.

The buyer can require the seller's cooperation with the investigation. The standards and procedures of the audit should be specifically set out in the sales contract. The agreement should also give the buyer the option of terminating the contract upon the discovery of a hazardous waste problem.

Title insurance generally does not protect real estate purchasers against hazardous waste liability.

Buyers should review records in both the U.S. District Court and the state court in the jurisdiction in which the property is located to find out if it is burdened with any existing state or federal hazardous waste liens because these liens may not be recorded in local (county or state) recorder of deed offices.

Finally, the buyer should seek indemnification provisions that will hold the seller liable for any costs related to unforseen hazardous waste problems. The government can and will sue any of the four categories of "responsible parties" for clean-up costs. An indemnification clause, however, can establish the right of the buyer eventually to recover liability costs from the seller. An indemnification clause should include out-of-pocket costs and should not place a dollar cap or time limit on the indemnification. Builders should pay careful attention to the seller's financial ability to back the provisions. If the parties agree on a specific monetary amount for which the seller will be responsible, the buyer may consider requiring the seller to post a bond for the duration of the expected cleanup.

Figure 3-2. Steps for Recognizing a Contaminated Site

- Inspect the property and surrounding area.
- Note any discolored or defoliated soils, odors, or chemical drums and containers.
- Look for storage tanks and industrial, mechanical, and electrical equipment.
- Investigate the historical use of the property:
- Has the property been the site of commercial or industrial use?
- Has it ever been used as a landfill or storage area?
- Are hazardous waste problems common to the area?
- Consult with local, state, and federal environmental agencies to determine if the site is on a list of properties suspected of contamination or awaiting cleanup.
- Check for government permits issued to current or past owners indicating the use of toxic chemicals.
- Review records in both the U.S. District Court and state court for the jurisdiction in which the property is located to find out if the property is incumbered by any existing state or federal liens.

3-1. Inspection Provisions and Option To Terminate Contract

Comments

Buyers should incorporate into their land purchase agreements a provision that allows additional time, if needed, to conduct an environmental audit. A buyer may decide, after physical inspection of the property or a review of the chain-of-title, that toxins may have been disposed of on the site and that a further study should be conducted to verify or discount this suspicion. Three options are provided in the sample language below.

Sample Language

Option 1—The buyer may ______ [at any time prior to closing of title; for____days following the execution of this contract,] enter upon the premises for the purposes of investigating the property or conducting an environmental audit to determine whether hazardous waste or toxic substances are present on the site. The terms, ***hazardous waste*** or ***toxic substances*** in this agreement have the same meaning that they have in these state and federal laws:______(list the laws)______.

If the inspection discloses the presence of an amount of

hazardous waste or toxic substances that the seller is unwilling to correct to the satisfaction of the buyer, the buyer or seller may cancel this contract and all rights of both parties under the contract shall cease. The cancelling party must personally serve a written notice of cancellation upon the other party or the other party's attorneys.

The seller shall return to the buyer____ percent (___%) of the deposit [with interest at____ percent (___%) per annum)] Costs and damages shall be allocated as follows: ____________________

Option 2—The seller hereby grants to the buyer, and the buyer's agents and employees the right to enter the property or any portion thereof (at any time prior to the closing of the title; for ____ days following the execution of this contract) for the purpose of conducting at the buyer's own cost any soil, geologic, engineering, and environmental investigations that the buyer may desire.

If any of these investigations disclose the presence of an amount of hazardous waste or toxic substances that the seller is unwilling to correct to the satisfaction of the buyer, the buyer or the seller may cancel this contract and all rights of both parties under the contract shall cease. The cancelling party must personally serve a written notice of cancellation upon the other party or the other party's attorneys.

The buyer agrees to indemnify and hold the seller harmless from any costs or liability incurred by any investigations conducted pursuant to this provision and, if this contract is voided for any reason not caused by the seller, the buyer shall, at the written request of the seller, repair any damages caused to the property by these investigations.

Option 3—The buyer shall promptly cause (designate testing facility), the testing facility, to inspect and, if necessary, test the soil, subsoil, water, and air conditions of the property to ascertain whether the property contains hazardous waste or toxic substances. The testing facility shall determine the number and quality of tests required to ascertain the presence or absence of hazardous waste or substances. The buyer agrees to furnish a copy of the report of the testing facility to the seller on or before (date) If the report indicates that in the judgment of the testing facility, the property contains hazardous waste or toxic substances, the buyer shall have the option to terminate this agreement. The buyer shall deliver written notice of the option to terminate to the seller within ______ days of receipt of the report of the testing facility. Costs and damages will be allocated as follows: ____________________.

3-2. Cooperation from Seller

Comments

The buyer may want to include in the contract a provision obligating the seller to cooperate in an investigation of the property.

Sample Language

The seller agrees to sign and execute any and all documents that may be required by any person, firm, partnership, company, or local, state or federal agency as a part of conducting an environmental audit of the property to determine the presence or absence of hazardous waste or toxic substances.

3-3. Seller Warranties

Comments

If the seller warrants that no hazardous substances are on the property, but they are present and the buyer becomes liable for cleanup costs, the buyer can recover those costs from the seller. The contract should specify that the warranty in the contract will survive the closing.

Sample Language

The seller warrants that the use, maintenance, operation, or condition of the property complies with all regulations, statutes, rules, and codes of all local, state, and federal governmental agencies having jurisdiction over the property.

The seller further warrants that the property does not contain any hazardous waste or toxic substances that may create liability for the purchaser or its agents, heirs, or assigns under local, state, or federal laws.

The provisions of this contract of sale will survive the real estate closing and shall not be merged with the deed.

3-4. Indemnification from Seller

Comments

The buyer also may be able to negotiate a specific provision in the contract that allocates responsibility to the seller for any liability imposed on the buyer for hazardous waste cleanup costs.

Sample Language

The seller agrees to indemnify and hold the buyer harmless from any costs or liability incurred by the buyer or the buyer's agents, heirs, or assigns for damages paid to any local, state, or federal agency or other government or private entities for costs of cleaning up hazardous waste or toxic substances. Damages include the actual cleanup costs incurred, and any legal or litigation costs and attorneys' fees related to the cleanup.

Radon Liability

All parties to a real estate transaction should be concerned about the problem of naturally occurring radioactive radon. Radon is a basic chemical element, like oxygen or carbon; no one can be blamed for its existence. But the lack of blame in the everyday sense of the word carries little weight in today's courtroom.

Although radon can be found in every home in the country and in the outside air, it has been called by some a more serious health threat than asbestos, formaldehyde, and toxic wastes. The only known health impact from radon is an increased risk of developing lung cancer. But the extent of this risk posed by normal indoor levels of radon is disputed. Debating the health-risk and policy questions surrounding radon is beyond the scope of this *Guide*. While these questions remain unanswered, builders should understand that they can be sued by home buyers if "elevated" levels of radon are found in a home. This section discusses ways the builder can deal with potential radon liability.

Claims against builders arising out of high radon levels found in homes can be brought under many different legal theories, including breach of express and implied warranties, negligence, strict liability, fraud and misrepresentation, and a host of other ways of assessing the liability of a defendant. These theories are based on state law and the reader should consult local attorneys for an explanation of the specific laws in their jurisdictions and to determine whether the suggested contract language in this *Guide* addresses their specific state laws.

With all of these theories, home buyers will have the difficult task of linking a specific personal injury with exposure to radon. That is, they will have difficulty proving in court that the radon in a particular home caused the homeowner's injury. However, a court could accept merely the increased risk to health posed by radon as the legal injury even if the homeowner exhibits no manifestation in the form of actual injury. In addition, in some states homeowners have no need to show physical injury to recover for mental anguish and emotional distress.

A buyer's own negligence that contributes to the injury, such as smoking or the failure to maintain a radon mitigation system, may prevent or limit a builder's liability. Plaintiffs must also comply with applicable statutes of limitations, the time within which someone must file a suit. Both sides should recognize that this litigation will be expensive and unpredictable. The cost of correcting a radon problem in most homes ($200 to $2,000) is small in comparison to the expense of a lawsuit.

3-5. Reducing the Legal Risks

While much potential radon liability exists, builders can take the steps listed in Figure 3-3 to reduce the risks.

3-6. Radon and Real Estate Transactions

Builders who have provided specific warnings or notices in their contracts can control liability for a buyer's claim of fraud or misrepresentation for failure to warn about unsafe conditions. Some buyers may not enter into a contract if they see this language because they may wrongly assume that, since the contract has a radon notice, the house is "hot" while the builder down the street who does not have a radon notice must have a "safe" house. The builder must develop an effective notice that does not scare off buyers.

While providing a radon notice provision in a contract is the prudent thing to do, a notice and the general concern over radon may breed demands for a radon inspection and sales contingency clause. But, if builders and buyers understand the dynamics of radon entry into a building and the problems with short-term radon tests, they should conclude that short-term inspection and contract contingencies are not in the parties' best interests. Therefore, the parties to a real estate contract should not allow the sale to be contingent on short term (3 to 7 days) radon test results.

The EPA's evaluation of radon levels and associated health risks is based on the average annual level of radon in a home and a lifetime (70 years) of exposure to those levels. In most cases, a short-term screening measurement of radon levels is not a reliable measure of the average annual level.

Short-term tests cannot provide accurate estimates of long-term health risks because radon levels fluctuate on a daily, weekly, and seasonal basis, sometimes by as much as 10-fold swings. Therefore, short-term test results only indicate whether longer term (3 months to 1 year) testing should be conducted.

According to the EPA, a short-term test that reveals a radon level between 4 and 20 picoCuries per liter (pCi/1) means that the occupant should conduct a long-term test within a year (to determine the annual average level and the risk to health). Why should anyone (seller, buyer, agent, or lender) base a decision about a real estate transaction on information that provides no useful estimate of the potential risk to the occupants health? Moreover, a testing contingency in a contract provides no additional liability protection for any of the parties, assuming an effective notice is provided as explained above. The issues of contract contingencies and radon inspections—while they should not be a factor in the liability equation—become consumer relations and business judgment decisions.

The EPA recommends that homeowners take remedial action within several weeks when their short-term screening test reveals levels at or greater than 200 pCi/1. Therefore, a contingency could be given to buyers for test results at these high levels. However, some technical experts suggest that even if a short-term test reveals much lower levels than 200 pCi/1, down to 50 or 20 pCi/1, that the annual average will probably be above 4 pCi/1. Therefore, the builder may want to provide a contingency in the contract if a short-term test reveals greater than 20 pCi/1 or some other mutually agreeable number. However, until measurement methods progress to the point where accurate health risk estimates can be made from short-term tests, contract contingencies based on the results of a short-term screening test are imprudent for all concerned.

Soil tests designed to predict radon levels that could occur in a building constructed on the site also are not recommended. A soil test that shows a low radon gas level does not indicate with a reasonable degree of assurance (from a liability perspective) that homes built on such soils will have low radon levels. Moreover, a proper site survey, requiring multiple soil test samples, can be more expensive than the cost of construction techniques to prevent or mitigate radon. Builders should compare the cost and usefulness of any soil test proposals with the cost and benefits of radon prevention techniques that are constructed into homes before committing to soil tests.

An escrow provision usually does not help the buyer because, if the market will bear it, a prudent seller will simply inflate the price of the house to cover the cost of the escrow. The Environmental Protection Agency estimates that up to 10 percent of the homes in this country are over 4 pCi/l on an annual average basis. Given these numbers, approximately 90 percent of all buyers would pay for something they may not need if escrows are routinely required.

Figure 3-3. Steps for Reducing Builders' Radon Liability Risks

• Builders should use construction methods that the technical experts say will help to prevent radon from entering homes.

• Builders and buyers should know, however, that while some good preliminary research has been produced, the industry is at the beginning of a learning curve on this whole issue. No one knows exactly what works, and no construction technique is foolproof. Also, some techniques may add significant cost to the price of a home—which is no small matter when extrapolated to the national housing market—and most require homeowner maintenance. Builders should contact the Technology and Codes Department of the National Association of Home Builders or the Environmental Protection Agency for the latest guidance on new home radon construction techniques.

• A specific notice regarding radon or indoor air quality should be included in the contract. An effective notice should (a) eliminate potential fraud and misrepresentation claims and (b) prevent potential negligence suits based on a failure to warn. However, the contract for a real estate transaction should not contain a contingency based on short-term (3 to 7 days) radon test results (see "3-6, Radon and Real Estate Transactions").

• Builders should not give any warranties that would cover radon. To expect builders or sellers of real estate to guarantee that a certain home will be "safe" from naturally occurring radon is unreasonable because the actual level of radon in a specific home depends on several factors that have nothing to do with the construction type, such as the occupants living habits and weather conditions. An express warranty should be quite specific. It should enumerate each item or condition that the builder intends to warrant. General or broad terms (as in any contract provision) should be avoided.

• Builders should disclaim or waive all warranties, expressed or implied, that are not specifically enumerated in the builder's limited express warranty. While some states will not enforce this disclaimer as to implied warranties, about 20 states have specifically allowed the disclaimer, and the trend toward allowing the disclaimer is increasing with the recognition of the harshness of the implied warranty rule on the builder. The disclaimer language should be simple, clear, and conspicuous (for example, in bold face type or in a box).

• The important point with all warranty provisions is for builders to be sincere with potential buyers, to let them know exactly what is warranted and what is not. The warranty should not leave any room for interpretation by either party, a judge, or a jury.

• Builders should negotiate an "indemnification and hold harmless" clause in their contracts with foundation and ventilation subcontractors and design professionals in order to pass on any remaining liability to more responsible parties.

Lenders and others need not be as concerned with radon as they justifiably are with respect to potential liability for asbestos contamination in a building or hazardous waste cleanup liability under the federal and state superfund laws. Unlike these other pollutants, high levels of radon can be reduced at a relatively low cost. The worst-case estimate for mitigation costs for a home runs up to $2,000 in 1990 dollars. While this is a substantial sum for most homeowners, the average is more likely to be down between $200 and $500. High radon levels do not lower the value of property nor do the potential costs of mitigation in comparison with the price of a house create any real potential for default on a mortgage.

3-7. Radon Contract Provisions

Comments

As was previously noted, builders should not use these sample contract provisions without consulting an attorney experienced in construction contract law because of the differences among the state laws. Builders' attorneys may advise not including one or more of these provisions or parts of them in their contracts for various reasons. Their attorneys also may advise combining various parts of the three provisions into one. The language in brackets [ ] is not part of the contract provision but is a note to the reader on ways the provision could be modified.

Sample Language

Option 1—Radon Notice and Disclaimer—The United States Environmental Protection Agency (EPA) and the ____(name the state)____ Department of Health or Environmental Protection have expressed concern over the presence of radon gas in homes. Prolonged exposure to high levels of indoor radon or its progeny may affect the health of residents. Although such conditions may exist, the builder has made no investigation to determine whether radon gas or other environmental pollutants are present in the home or affecting the premises. The builder has made no analysis or verification of the extent of the environmental or health hazard, if any, that may affect the premises or residents.

The builder makes no representation or warranty as to the presence or lack of radon or hazardous environmental condition, nor as to the effect of radon or any such condition on the premises or residents.

> The builder further disclaims and buyer waives—unless otherwise expressly provided for in the builder's limited warranty—all warranties, express or implied, including but not limited to the warranties of good workmanship, habitability, merchantability, and fitness of purpose, and including any warranties that could be construed to cover the presence of radon or other environmental pollutants. The only warranties the builder provides to the buyer are those contained in the limited warranty.

Option 2—Radon Notice—Radon is a naturally occurring gas that is caused by the radioactive decay of the element radium. Since radium is contained in the earth's crust and dissolves readily in water, radon can be found virtually everywhere. Preliminary studies suggest that prolonged indoor exposure to high levels of radon gas may result in adverse health consequences.

This notice serves to advise the purchaser that above average levels of radon gas may accumulate in any home, regardless of the type of home or who builds it. Specific radon levels depend on an array of factors, including site-specific variables such as soil type and conditions, wind and climate conditions, geology and groundwater, and building-specific variables such as:

- Construction materials and techniques;]
- Age of the structure;
- Heating, ventilating and air conditioning systems; and
- Occupant upkeep and living habits.

In addition, indoor radon levels can fluctuate on a yearly, seasonal, or even daily basis.

Because of the multitude of factors involved, predicting whether a residence may be subject to high radon levels is difficult, unless tests to determine actual radon concentrations are conducted on a completed structure. The United States Environmental Protection Agency (EPA) and the Department of Energy are conducting extensive investigations regarding this matter.

The EPA has issued testing protocols that radon testing firms and home owners should follow when testing homes. Home buyers may wish to make arrangements to test their homes for radon. Costs for radon test kits vary from $10 to $50 or more. EPA publishes a list of EPA-approved suppliers of such test kits. If a home buyer decides to measure the level of radon gas in a home and if the tests detect an elevated level, the home buyer may wish to take steps to conduct longer-term testing or to reduce the level detected.

If the builder has utilized sub-slab ventilation, the contract can state here:

One step the buyer may wish to take is to install or have installed a small ventilation fan as recommended by EPA to vent gas from beneath the slab. The builder has prepared this home for the addition of a sub-slab ventilation system. The buyer may wish to contact EPA or the state's environmental protection office for further information on whether to install such a fan and on the choice of a fan. (EPA Regional Office address and phone number and the address and phone number of the applicable state office).

Alternatively, the builder may offer to test the home, at the buyer's expense, by stating:

At closing the builder shall deliver to the buyer a certificate from a firm that participates in the EPA's Radon Measurement Proficiency Program indicating what level of radon was present in the home at the time of the screening. The buyer acknowledges that the builder has not independently gathered any of the information that is contained within the certificate and that the builder is merely providing the buyer with information that has been made available to it by an independent firm. The buyer further acknowledges that the builder is not warranting the accuracy of the screening or the information contained within the certificate. Any rescreening of the residence or update of the certificate shall be performed by the buyer at the buyer's sole expense (see also the "No Contingency" clause printed below).

The buyer acknowledges that the builder does not claim or possess any special expertise in the measurement or reduction of radon, nor does the builder provide any advice to the buyer as to acceptable levels or possible health hazards of the gas.

If the builder uses radon construction techniques, the contract may state:

The builder has relied on the expertise of the government agencies that have been studying this issue and, the builder has constructed the home with the following techniques, as recommended by *Radon Reduction in New Construction: An Interim Guide*:* (describe construction techniques such as sub-slab ventilation, extra caulking, and others). Since no construction technique is known to be foolproof, the builder assumes no responsibility for the operation, maintenance, or effectiveness of sub-slab ventilation systems or any other devices or methods intended for the reduction of radon gas levels.

Sample Language

Option 3—Contract Not Contingent on Radon—The United States Environmental Protection Agency (EPA) does not have mandatory regulations regarding radon levels in homes. However, the EPA has issued A *Citizen's Guide To Radon*, (which the purchaser acknowledges receiving from the builder [/].) (buyers' initials). This *Guide* explains what the owner of a home should do upon receiving the results of a radon test.

Radon is measured in terms of picoCuries per liter (pCi/1). The EPA discussion of pCi/1, its suggested actions, and its estimates of risk to health are based on the average annual level of radon in a home. In most cases, a short-term (3 to 7 days) test of radon levels is not a reliable measure of the average annual level.

Therefore, buyers agree that this contract is not contingent on radon testing results or the presence or lack of radon in the home. The buyers further agree that they shall not extend the closing date or withhold from the builder any payment or any portion thereof of the contract price for any reason, including radon test results or the presence of radon in the home. By closing the purchase of the property, the buyer will be deemed to have released the builder from any and all claims and liabilities relating to or arising from the presence of radon or other environmental hazards on the property and from any and all responsibility for mitigating any elevated levels of radon gas or other environmental hazards that may be discovered on the property.

---

*OPA-87-009 (Washington, D.C: U.S. Environmental Protection Agency, 1987).

4

General Building Specifications

The general building specification should be prepared as a separate document and referenced along with other documents, such as blueprints, plans, and architectural drawings in the contract (see Section 2-2, "The Contract Documents," in Chapter 2, "The Contract Between Builder and Buyer or Owner"). The specifications should state that they cover labor and materials for construction of a specific building at the new home address, and they should include a legal description of the property as it appears in the Contract (see Section 2-1, "Caption," in chapter 2. The specifications should be as detailed as possible, reference the plans and blueprints where appropriate, and include provisions for the items listed in Figure 4-1. This list is provided only as an example. Other necessary parts of the construction process may not be listed here, and some of the listed items may not apply to a particular project. All work must be listed and described on the specifications document.

Figure 4-1. Items Usually Included in Specifications

Excavation and land conditions
Backfilling and grading
Footings
Basement floor or slab
Foundation walls
Stoops
Chimneys
Steel columns and girders
Masonry or frame exterior walls
Walks and driveways
Floor framing and subflooring
Finish flooring
Wall finishing (specify for each room)]
Bath fixtures
Partition studs
Ceiling framing
Roof system, sheathing, built-up roofing, and roofing materials
Drywall or plaster
Exterior doors and trim
Windows
Interior doors and trim
Cabinets
Stairs
Plumbing
Electric wiring and fixtures
Heating and air-conditioning
Gutters, downspouts, flashing, other sheet metal work
Insulation
Painting and decorating
Finish hardware
Appliances
Garages, carports
Landscaping and planting
Miscellaneous

5

Warranties and Disclaimers

Express and Implied Warranties

To a large extent, a builder's liability depends on the warranties that the builder gives to home buyers. Every time a builder, the builder's agents, or employees make a promise to a buyer, they may be extending a warranty. This fact applies to any representations made in advertisements or brochures. Warranties do not have to be in writing. An *express warranty* is treated by the courts like any other agreement, and if a builder breaches a warranty, it is like breaching a contract.

In addition to express warranties, courts have found implied warranties in contracts to construct new homes. Even if builders make no statement or express promises, written or verbal, about the condition of the houses, many courts assume that they have provided an "implied warranty of habitability and fitness," meaning that they have promised to provide a house that is habitable and suitable for its intended purpose.

Some courts also assume that the builders are providing an *implied warranty* of good workmanship," whether or not the contracts to build houses expressly promise to provide it. These implied warranties are dangerous because the courts—not the parties to the contract—determine what is covered by the warranties.

In theory, since a warranty is like any other promise in a contract, the builder should be able to write a contract disclaiming or limiting any warranties, even implied warranties. In an increasing number of states, the courts have enforced contract provisions in which the parties agree to waive implied warranties. In other states, however, courts have stated (a) that consumers need special protection purchasing their homes, which often are their most expensive investments, and (b) that they must not be allowed to waive the implied warranties.

However, disclaiming all implied warranties involves risks:

• The trend is toward including more items within the reach of the Magnuson-Moss Warranty Act (see below), and if builders offer a full express warranty they cannot limit implied warranties under the Act.

• Some courts will not uphold a contract provision that is deemed "unconscionable" or unfair and overreaching to the consumer.

• Some builders have found that from a marketing perspective providing a limited warranty that restricts the duration of the implied warranties makes better business sense than to eliminate all implied warranties.

The Federal Government regulates warranties on consumer products under the Magnuson-Moss Warranty Act[5-1] The Act does not require a builder to give a warranty. It merely regulates the form of whatever warranty a builder may voluntarily decide to give. The Act states that these warranties must meet certain disclosure requirements if they are to be valid. These requirements do not apply to new houses themselves, but only to the following items that are installed or included in a new house: appliances, manufactured equipment, and anything else defined as a consumer product under the Act.

The builder's warranty provisions that cover consumer products must be written according to Federal Trade Commission regulations.

Builders are faced with three choices when considering their responsibilities under the Magnuson-Moss Act:

• They can give no warranty at all, which may not be a practical alternative in most markets.

• They can exclude consumer products entirely from their warranty and, thereby, avoid triggering the Magnuson-Moss requirements. However, builders should keep in mind that an enormous variety of appliances and pieces of equipment will be excluded.

5-1. See *A Primer for Builders . . .New Home Warranties and the Magnuson-Moss Warranty Act* (Washington, D.C.: National Association of Home Builders, 1978), available from the NAHB Consumer Affairs Department.

• They can conform their warranties to Magnuson-Moss guidelines.

If any part of a builder's warranty is covered by Magnuson-Moss and the builder provides for alternative dispute resolution of claims, the warranty must follow the settlement procedures outlined in the Act. Therefore, builders should provide for alternative dispute resolution in a separate provision (see Section 2-11, "Arbitration" in Chapter 2, "Contract Between Builder and Buyer or Owner").

The Magnuson-Moss Act does not allow builders to disclaim implied warranties on consumer products if they give a written warranty (see "Limited Warranties" later in this chapter). If builders follow the Magnuson-Moss Act guidelines for limited warranties they are permitted to restrict the duration of the implied warranties (unless state law does not permit the restriction). The requirements are fairly simple and are designed merely to make warranties more understandable to consumers. Some courts are more likely to enforce a limited warranty if it is simple, clear, and easy for a home buyer to understand even if the Magnuson-Moss Act does not specifically apply.

Under the Federal Trade Commission (FTC) regulations, the warranty document must include the information in Figure 5-1. Additional information on Magnuson-Moss appears in the FTC advisory opinion in Figure 5-2.

Figure 5-1. Federal Trade Regulation Requirements for Warranty Documents

• The name of the person who is receiving the warranty and whether it is transferable to subsequent purchasers

• Precisely what the warranty covers and what is excluded

• What the builder will do if a warranted defect or problem occurs, and how much the consumer will be charged

• The duration of the warranty and when it begins

• The procedures a buyer must follow to have a problem corrected

• Limitations on consequential or secondary results must stand out from the rest of the document, and they must be followed by these exact words: "Some states do not allow the exclusion or limitation of incidental or consequential damages, so the above limitation or exclusion may not apply to you."

• Any limitations on the duration of implied warranty rights also must appear conspicuously on the face of the warranty, along with the statement: "Some states do not allow limitations on how long an implied warranty lasts, so this limitation may not apply to you."

• A provision stating: "This warranty gives you specific legal rights, and you may also have other rights which vary from state to state."

Limited Warranty

The language of any written warranty provided by the builder to the buyer may determine the extent of liability of the builder. Although the language is simple, it has legal effect. As explained in the opening of this chapter, builders should use a limited express warranty that restricts the duration of implied warranties. After evaluating the risks previously outlined in this chapter, builders should consider totally disclaiming all implied warranties in those states that permit it. A full or whole express warranty is not recommended because, under the Magnuson-Moss Act, builders cannot limit implied warranties at all if they provide a full, written warranty.

This section includes two alternative limited warranty agreements (Figures 5-3 and 5-4) and a statement of nonwarrantable conditions (Figure 5-5). Builders should not use these provisions without consulting an attorney experienced in building industry warranties and revising them to fit the facts of each situation. They should read the preceding portion of this chapter to understand the significance of the language contained in these limited warranties. They also must coordinate the warranties they use with Sections 2-13, "Inspections, Acceptance, and Possession," and 2-16, "Representations and Warranty," in Chapter 2, "Contract Between Builder and Buyer or Owner." (Sample language for a limited warranty agreement excluding items covered by the Magnuson-Moss Act appears in Figure 5-3, and a sample limited warranty agreement conforming to the Magnuson-Moss act appears in Figure 5-4. Figure 5-5 contains a sample statement of nonwarrantable conditions.)

Builders who participate in insured warranty programs should redraft or disregard the language here to avoid conflict with the insured warranty program.

Figure 5-2. Federal Trade Commission Advisory Opinion to the National Association of Home Builders

(Listed below are the questions and answers provided to the National Association of Home Builders by the Federal Trade Commission in its advisory opinion concerning Sections 102(b) and 111(d) of the Magnuson-Moss Act, 15 U.S.C. sec. 2301 et seq., and the Commission's rule on the Pre-Sale Availability of Written Warranty Terms, 16 C.F.R. sec. 702, as they apply to the homebuilding industry. The exemption ruling [questions 1-3 and advisory opinion [questions 4-8 appear in a June 21, 1978, letter from the Federal Trade Commission to NAHB's general counsel.)

Questions

1. When a builder gives the purchaser an allowance to select various fixtures or appliances (consumer products) from a third party supplier, is it the builder or the third party supplier who must comply with the pre-sale availability of warranties requirements for "sellers" under 16 C.F.R. 702.3(a) in each of the following situations?

A. The purchaser makes selections from stock purchased wholesale by, and in the possession of, the builder, and makes payment to the builder for any items selected in excess of the allowance.

B. The purchaser makes selections in the showroom of the builder's supplier, from items not yet purchased by the builder and makes payment to the builder for any items selected in excess of the allowance.

C. The purchaser makes selections from items not yet purchased by the builder and makes payment directly to the supplier for any item selected in excess of the allowance.

Answers

1A. When a builder gives a purchaser an allowance to select consumer products, and the purchaser makes selections directly from the builder's stock, the builder must comply with the seller's duties under 16 C.F.R. 702.3(a) to make warranty terms available prior to sale.

1B and C. When a builder gives a purchaser an allowance to select consumer products from the stock of builder's supplier, the builder is exempted from compliance with 16 C.F.R. 702.3(a). In this latter situation, the builder's supplier is also not required to comply with the seller's pre-sale duties under the rule if the supplier's sales are totally wholesale, including builder referred sales.

Questions

2. What are a custom builder's duties as a "seller" under 16 C.F.R. 702 when the purchaser can choose from among virtually all brands of appliances available in the market-place?

Answers

2. When a purchaser contracts to have a custom home built, and pursuant to the contract can choose appliances from among virtually all of those available in the market-place, the builder is exempted from compliance with the seller's duties under 16 C.F.R. 702.3(a) to make the text of written warranties available prior to sale.

3. If the builder has made the pre-sale warranty information available to the purchaser for all appliances from which the purchaser can choose, does the builder have any obligation under 16 C.F.R. 702 to make warranty information available, after a contract is signed, for substitute appliances which the purchaser must select due to a manufacturer's discontinuation or replacement of the appliance initially chosen by the purchaser?

3. A builder must make warranty terms available for inspection by a purchaser if, after a contract is signed, the purchaser must make a second selection because originally selected items have become unavailable. The builder is not exempted from compliance with 16 C.F.R. 702.3(a) in this situation.

4. Does the Magnuson-Moss Warranty Act require that all builders' warranties on consumer products contain a clause assigning the manufacturers' warranties to the purchaser, or does the Act have the effect of automatically making all manufacturer's warranties on such appliances run to the ultimate purchaser?

4. The Magnuson-Moss Warranty Act does not govern the issue of whether a manufacturer's warranty on a consumer product must be assigned by a builder to the home purchaser. This question is governed by state law.

Figure 5-2. Federal Trade Commission Advisory Opinion to the National Association of Home Builders

Questions	Answers
5. Is the builder or the purchaser the proper party to complete and return the warranty registration cards?	5. Registration cards would be prohibited under the commission's rule for Reasonable Duties Under a Full Warranty, as proposed in 43 *Fed. Reg.* 39223 (August 3, 1977); see also the Commission's Interpretations of the Act, 16 C.F.R.700.7(b).]However, registration cards are permitted for limited warranties. When a limited warranty offered on a consumer product by a manufacturer includes the registration card, the home purchaser is the proper party to complete and return the card, unless the warranty specifically requries this of retailers.
6. Does Section 111(d) of the Magnuson-Moss Warranty Act exempt the mandatory FHA/VA warranty from the requirements of the Magnuson-Moss Act?	6. Section 111(d) of the Magnuson-Moss Warranty Act exempts the mandatory FHA/VA warranty offered by a builder from the requirements of the Act (except for Section 102(c)).
7. Is a builder who gives only the mandatory FHA/VA warranty required to comply with 16 C.F.R. 702 for those consumer products sold with warranties that are covered by the Act?	7. A builder who gives only the mandatory FHA/VA warranty must still make available under 16 C.F.R. 702 those warranties that are covered by the Act; the fact that the FHA/VA warranty is generally exempt from the Act does not affect the builder's status as a "seller" of consumer products sold with warranties that are covered by the act.

Questions	Answers
If a builder gives both the mandatory FHA/VA warranty and voluntarily offers an additional warranty not required by any federal law (e.g., a one-year warranty against defects in materials and workmanship), to what extent is the additional warranty subject to the Magnuson-Moss Warranty Act.?	8. Any warranty offered by a builder on a consumer product that is not required by federal law is subject to the provisions of the Magnuson-Moss Warranty Act.

Figure 5-3. Sample Limited Warranty Agreement That Excludes Items Covered by the Magnuson Moss Act

This limited warranty agreement is extended by ____ ______(builder's name)______ (the builder), whose address is______ ______(builder's address)______ to___(buyer's name)___ (the buyer), who ___[is/are]___ the original buyer(s) of the property at the following address (house):______________________

____

____

____

____

____

This limited warranty excludes consequential damages, limits the duration of implied warranties, and provides for liquidated damages.

1. What Is Covered by the Warranty

The builder warrants that all construction related to the house substantially conforms with the plans and specifications and change orders for this job. The builder warrants that during the first 30 days after the buyer moves in, the builder will adjust or correct minor defects, omissions, or malfunctions, such as missing equipment or hardware; sticking doors, drawers, and windows; dripping faucets; and other minor malfunctions reported by the buyer upon inspection of the property.

Within one year from the date of closing or occupancy by the buyer, whichever is first, the builder will repair or replace, at the builder's option, any latent defects in material or workmanship by the standards of construction relevant in ______(city, state)______. A *latent defect* is defined as one which was not (apparent/ascertainable) at the time of occupancy. The buyer agrees to accept a reasonable match in any repair or replacement in the event the original item is no longer available.

2. What Is Not Covered

This limited warranty does not cover—

A. Damage resulting from fires, floods, storms, electrical malfunctions, accidents, nor acts of God;

B. Damage from alterations, misuse or abuse of the covered items by any person;

C. Damage resulting from the buyer's failure to observe any operating instructions furnished by the builder at the time of installation;

D. Damage resulting from a malfunction of equipment or lines of the telephone, gas, power, or water companies;

E. Any items listed as "Nonwarrantable Conditions" on the list that is incorporated into this contract; the buyer acknowledges receipt of the list of "Nonwarrantable Conditions" ________/________;
(buyers' initials)

F. Any item furnished or installed by the buyer; nor

G. Any appliance, piece of equipment, or other item that is a consumer product for the purposes of the Magnuson-Moss Warranty Act, 15 U.S.C. Sec. 2301 et seq., installed or included in the buyer's property. The only warranties of items listed below are those that the manufacturer provides to the buyer:[5-2]

Roofing	Kitchen appliances	Mixer
Brick	Refrigerator	Light fixtures
Siding	Microwave	Floor coverings
Plumbing fixtures	Ovens	Windows
Heating equipment	Stove	Doors
Cooling equipment	Sink	
Water heater	Garbage disposal	

(1) The builder has made any such warranties available to the buyer for the buyer's inspection and the buyer acknowledges receipt of copies of any warranties requested.

________/________
(buyers' initials)

(2) The builder hereby assigns (to the extent that they are assignable) and conveys to the buyer all warranties provided to the builder on any manufactured items that have been installed or included in the buyer's property. The buyer accepts this assignment and acknowledges that the builder's only responsibility relating to such items is to lend assistance to the buyer in settling any claim resulting from the installation of these products.________/________ ________________
(buyers' initials) (builder's initials)

3. Remedies and Limitations

A. The buyer understands that the sole remedies under this limited warranty agreement are repair and replacement as set forth here.________/________
(buyers' initials)

B. With respect to any claim whatsoever asserted by the buyer against the builder, the buyer understands that the buyer will have no right to recover or request compensation for, and the builder shall not be liable for any—

(1) Incidental, consequential, secondary, or punitive damages;

(2) Damages for aggravation, mental anguish, emotional distress, or pain and suffering; nor

(3) Attorney's fees or costs.________/________
(buyers' initials)

C. The builder hereby limits the duration of all implied warranties, including the implied warranties of fitness of purpose, habitability, and workmanlike construction to one year from

5-2. **Warning**—This list is not exclusive. Builders should consult *A Primer for Builders...New Home Warranties and the Magnuson-Moss Act* (Washington, D.C.: National Association of Home Builders, 1978); available from the NAHB Consumer Affairs Department.

Figure 5-3. Sample Limited Warranty Agreement That Excludes Items Covered by the Magnuson Moss Act (cont.)

the date of sale or the date of occupancy, whichever comes first

D. These limitations shall be enforceable to the extent permitted by law. Some states do not allow the exclusion or limitation of incidental or consequential damages or the limitation of implied warranties, so the limitations or exclusions listed above may not apply.

Alternative to 3C

[C. The Buyer understands that no implied warranties whatsoever apply to the structure of the house and items that are functionally part of the house. The builder disclaims any implied warranties, including (but not limited to) warranties of habitability, fitness of purpose, and workmanlike construction, to the extent allowed by law, and any implied warranty that exists despite this disclaimer is limited to a period of one year. These limitations shall be enforceable to the extent permitted by the law. Some states do not allow limitations on how long an implied warranty lasts, so this limitation may not apply. ________/________
(buyers' initials)

[The buyer acknowledges acceptance of these limitations on the warranties offered by the builder in consideration for the limited warranty and the other provisions of the construction contract. The buyer, therefore, agrees to these limitations if, notwithstanding the provisions of the limited warranty, liability should arise on the part of the builder.]

D. Notwithstanding the provisions of this limited warranty agreement, if any liability arises on the part of the builder, the builder will pay the amount of actual provable damages arising from such liability, but the amount shall not exceed $ _______ This amount, fixed as liquidated damages and not as a penalty shall be the builder's complete and exclusive amount of liability. The provisions of this paragraph apply if loss or damage results directly or indirectly to persons or property from the performance or failure to perform obligations imposed by the construction contract, or from negligence, active or otherwise, of the builder, the builder's agents, or employees.

The buyer (a) understands that this provision limits the damages for which the builder will be liable and (b) acknowledges acceptance of this liquidated damages provision in consideration for the limited warranties provided by the builder and the other provisions of the construction contract. The buyer, therefore, agrees to this liquidated damages clause if, notwithstanding the provisions of this limited warranty, liability should arise on the part of the builder. ________/________
(buyers' initials)

E. This warranty is personal to the original buyer and does not run with the property or the items contained in the house. The original buyer may not assign, transfer, or convey this warranty without the prior written consent of the builder.

4. How To Obtain Service

If a problem develops during the warranty period, the buyer should notify the builder in writing at the address given above of the specific problem and what may need to be done about it. The written statement of the problem should include the buyer's name, address, telephone number, and a description of the nature of the problem. The builder will begin performing the obligations under this warranty within a reasonable time of the builder's receipt of such a request and will diligently pursue these obligations.

Repair work will be done during builder's normal working hours. The buyer agrees to provide the builder or builder's representative access to the house and the presence, during the work, of a responsible adult with the authority to approve repair and sign a call-back ticket upon completion of the repair.

5. Specific Legal Rights

This limited warranty gives the buyer specific legal rights, and the buyer may also have other rights which vary from state to state.

6. Where To Get Further Help

If the buyer wishes further help or information concerning this warranty, the buyer should contact the builder.

7.The Only Warranty Given by the Builder

The buyer acknowledges (a) that the buyer has thoroughly examined the property to be conveyed, (b) that the buyer relies solely on the buyer's judgment in signing this limited warranty, and (c) that the builder has made no guarantees, warranties, understandings, nor representations (nor have any been made by any representatives of the builder) that are not set forth in this document.

I/We acknowledge having read, understood, and received a copy of this limited warranty agreement.

____________________ (buyer)

____________________ (builder)

____________________ (buyer)

By____________________

Date____________________

Title____________________

Date____________________

Figure 5-4. Sample Limited Warranty Agreement Conforming to the Magnuson Moss Act

Warning—This warranty form must be adapted to conform to applicable state law. This form is only one possible form of warranty conforming to the Magnuson-Moss Act. Builders should consult their attorneys for a more complete discussion of a builder's duties under the Act and alternative language. Other language may provide more complete protection for the builder than is included here.

1. Consequential and Incidental Damages

Consequential and incidental damages are excluded, and the implied warranties are limited in duration.

2. Term

The terms of the various coverages of this warranty begin on the date of final settlement or the date when the buyer first occupies the home, whichever comes first.

3. Coverage

The builder warrants that by the standards of construction relevant in (city, state) for a period of one year:

A. The floors, ceilings, walls, and other internal structural components of the home that are not covered by other portions of this limited warranty will be free of defects in materials or workmanship;

B. The plumbing, heating, and electric wiring systems, and the septic tank (if the builder installed it) will be free of defects in materials or workmanship; and

C. The roof will be free of leaks caused by defects in materials or workmanship.

The builder warrants that by the standards of construction relevant in ________________ for a period of 60 days that the following items will be free of defects in materials or workmanship: doors (including hardware); windows; jalousies; electric switches, receptacles, and fixtures; caulking around exterior openings; plumbing figures; and cabinet work.

4. Manufacturers' Warranties

The builder assigns and passes through to the buyer (to the extent they are assignable), the manufacturers' warranties on all appliances and equipment. The following items are examples of such appliances and equipment, although not every home includes all of these items and some homes may include appliances or equipment not in this list: refrigerator, range, furnace or heat pump, washing machine, dishwasher, garbage disposal, ventilating fan, air-conditioner.

5. Exclusions from Coverage

The Builder does not assume responsibility for any of the following, all of which are excluded from the coverage of this limited warranty:

A. Consequential or incidental damages (Some states do not allow the exclusion or limitation of incidental or consequential damages, so the limitation or exclusion may not apply to you.);

B. Defects in appliances and equipment that are covered by manufacturers' warranties (The Builder has assigned these manufacturers' warranties to the buyer to the extent they are assignable, and the buyer should follow the procedures in these warranties if defects appear in these items.);

C. Damage resulting from ordinary wear and tear abusive use, or lack of proper maintenance of the home;

D. Defects that result from characteristics common to the materials used, such as (but not limited to) warping and deflection of wood; fading, chalking, and checking of paint from exposure to sunlight; cracks that occurred in the drying and curing of concrete, stucco, plaster, bricks, and masonry; drying, shrinking, and cracking of caulking and weather stripping;

E. Defects in items installed by the buyer or anyone other than the builder or, if requested by the builder, the builder's subcontractors;

F. Work done by the buyer or anyone other than the builder or, if requested by the builder, the builder's subcontractors;

G. Loss or injury attributable to the elements;

H. Conditions resulting from condensation on, or expansion or contraction of, materials;

I. Paint applied over newly plastered interior walls.[5-3]

6. No Other Warranties

This limited warranty is the only express warranty the builder gives. Implied warranties, including (but not limited to) warranties of merchantability, fitness for a particular purpose, habitability, and good workmanship are limited to the warranty period (term) set forth above. Some states do not allow limitations on how long an implied warranty lasts, so this limitation may not apply to you. This limited warranty gives you specific legal rights, and you may have other rights which vary from state to state.[5-4]

5-3. Builders should consult Section 6C, "Statement of Nonwarrantable Conditions," for further exclusions to be included here.

5-4. This limitation of implied warranties applies to only implied warranties on consumer products. If it is allowed by state law, builders can still exclude or disclaim all implied warranties on the house itself and any other items not considered consumer products under the Act.

Figure 5-4. Sample Limited Warranty Agreement Conforming to the Magnuson-Moss Act (cont.)

7. Claims Procedure

If a defect appears that the buyer thinks is covered by this limited warranty, the buyer must write a letter describing it to the builder at the builder's office address given above. The buyer must tell the builder in writing what times during the day that the buyer will be at home, so that the builder can schedule service calls appropriately. If a delay will cause extra damage (e.g., a pipe has burst), the buyer should telephone the builder. Only emergency reports will be taken by phone Failure to notify the builder of defects covered under this limited warranty or any implied warranties relieves the builder of all liability for replacement, repair, and all other damages.

8. Repairs

Upon receipt of the buyer's written report of a defect, if the defective item is covered by this warranty, the builder will repair or replace it at no charge to the buyer within 60 days (longer if weather conditions, labor problems, or material shortages cause delays). The work will be done by the builder or subcontractors chosen by the builder. The builder has sole discretion to choose between repair or replacement.

9. Not Transferable

This limited warranty is extended to the buyer only if the buyer is the first purchaser of the home. When the first purchaser sells the home or moves out of it, this limited warranty automatically terminates. It is not transferable to subsequent purchasers of the home nor to the first purchaser's tenants.

______________________ (buyer)	______________________ (builder)
______________________ (buyer)	By______________________
Date ______________________	Title ______________________
	Date ______________________

Figure 5-5. Sample Statement of Nonwarrantable Conditions

This statement of conditions that are not subject to the builder's warranties explains some of the changes and need for maintenance that may occur in a new home over the first year or so of occupancy. A home requires more maintenance and care than most products because it is made of many different components, each with its own special characteristics.

The buyer understands that like other products made by humans, a house is not perfect. It will show some minor flaws and unforeseeable defects, and it may require some adjustments and touching up.

As described in the limited warranty provided to the buyer of which this statement of "Nonwarrantable Conditions" is made a part, the builder will correct certain defects that arise during defined time periods after construction is completed. Other items that are not covered by the builder's warranty may be covered by manufacturers' warranties.

Some conditions, including (but not limited to) those listed in this statement of nonwarrantable conditions, are not covered under the builder's warranties. The buyer should read these carefully and understand that the buyer has not contracted for the builder to correct certain types of problems that may occur in the buyer's new house. These guidelines will alert the buyer to certain types of maintenance (a) that are the responsibility of the buyer and (b) that could lead to problems if they are neglected.

The following list outlines some of the conditions that are not warranted by the builder. The buyer should be sure to understand this list. If the buyer has any questions, the buyer should ask the builder and feel free to consult an attorney before signing the acknowledgement.

1. Concrete

Concrete foundations, walks, drives, and patios can develop hairlines cracks that do not affect the structural integrity of the building. These cracks are caused by characteristics of expansion and contraction. No method of eliminating these cracks exists. This condition does not affect the strength of the building.

2. Masonry and Mortar

Masonry and mortar can develop cracks from shrinkage of either the mortar or the brick. This condition is normal and should not be considered a defect.

3. Wood

Wood will sometimes check, crack, or "spread apart" because of the drying out process. This condition is most often caused by the heat inside the house or the exposure to the sun on the outside of the house. This condition is considered normal, and the homeowner is responsible for any maintenance or repairs resulting from it.

4. Sheetrock or Drywall

Sheetrock or drywall will sometimes develop nail pops or settlement cracks. These nail pops and settlement cracks are a normal part of the drying out process. These items can easily be handled by the homeowner with spackling during normal redecorating. However, if the homeowner wishes, the builder will send a worker at the end of one year to make the necessary repairs. Builders repairs will not include repainting.

5. Floor Squeaks

After extensive research and writing on the subject, technical experts have concluded that much has been tried but that little can be done about floor squeaks. Generally, floor squeaks will appear and disappear over time with changes in the weather.

6. Floors

Floors are not warranted for damage caused by neglect or the incidents of use. Wood, tile, and carpet all require maintenance. Floor casters are recommended to prevent scratching or chipping of wood or tile, and stains should be cleaned from carpets, wood, or tile immediately to prevent discoloration. Carpet has a tendency to loosen in damp weather and will stretch tight again in dryer weather.

7. Caulking

Exterior caulking and interior caulking in bathtubs, shower stalls, and ceramic tile surfaces will crack or bleed somewhat in the months after installation. These conditions are normal and should not be considered a problem. Maintenance or repairs resulting from them are the homeowner's responsibility.

8. Brick Discoloration

Most bricks may discolor because of the elements, rain runoff, weathering, or bleaching.

9. Broken Glass

Any broken glass or mirrors that are not noted by the buyer on the final inspection form are the responsibility of the buyer.

10. Frozen Pipes

The buyer must take precautions to prevent freezing of pipes and sillcocks during cold weather, such as removing outside hoses from sillcocks, leaving faucets with a slight drip, and turning off the water system if the house is to be left for extended periods during cold weather.

Figure 5-5. Sample Statement of Nonwarrantable Conditions (cont.)

11. Stained Wood

All items that are stained will normally have a variation of colors because of the different texture of the woods. Because of weather changes, doors that have panels will sometimes dry out and leave a small space of bare wood. These normal conditions should not be considered defects.

12. Paint

Good quality paint has been used internally and externally on this home. Nevertheless, exterior paint can sometimes crack or check. The source of this defect is most often something other than the paint. To avoid problems with the paint, buyers should avoid allowing lawn sprinklers to hit painted areas, washing down painted areas, and so on. Buyers should also not scrub latex-painted, inside walls and be careful of newly painted walls as they move furniture. The best paint will be stained or chipped if it is not cared for properly. Any defects in painting that are not noted at final inspection the responsibility of the buyer.

13. Cosmetic Items

The buyer has not contracted with the builder to cover ordinary wear and tear or other occurrences subsequent to construction that affect the condition of features in the home. Chips, scratches, or mars in tile, woodwork, walls, porcelain, brick, mirrors, plumbing fixtures, marble and formica tops, lighting fixtures, kitchen and other appliances, doors, paneling, siding, screens, windows, carpet, vinyl floors, cabinets, and the like that are not recognized and noted by the buyer at the final inspection are nonwarrantable conditions, and the upkeep of any cosmetic aspect of the home are the buyer's responsibility.

14. Plumbing

Dripping faucets, toilet adjustments, and toilet seats are covered by the builder's warranty for a _____ day period only. After that, they are the buyer's responsibility. If the plumbing is stopped up during the warranty period and the person servicing the plumbing finds foreign materials in the line, the buyer will be billed for the call.

15. Alterations to Grading

The buyer's lot has been graded to ensure proper drainage away from the home. Should the buyer wish to change the drainage pattern because of landscaping, installation of patio or service walks, or other reasons, the buyer should be sure a proper drainage slope is retained. The builder assumes no responsibility for the grading or subsequent flooding or stagnant pool formation if the established pattern is altered.

16. Lawn and Shrubs

The builder accepts no responsibility for the growth of grass or shrubs. Once the builder grades, seeds, and/or sods, and fertilizes the yard, the buyer must water and spread ground cover to prevent erosion. The builder will not regrade a yard, nor remove or replace any shrubs or trees, except for those that are noted as diseased at final inspection.

17. Roof Damage

The warranty on the buyer's roof is for material only and is prorated over the period of the lifetime use of the roof. Warranty claims for any defects in materials will be handled with the manufacturer with the builder's assistance.

The builder will not be responsible for any damages caused by walking on the roof or by installing a television antenna or other item on the roof.

18. Heating and Air-Conditioning

The buyer's source of heating and air-conditioning is covered by a manufacturer's warranty. The buyer is responsible for making sure the filters are kept clean and changed on a 30-day basis. Failure to do so may void the warranty. Having the equipment serviced or checked at least yearly is a good idea.

19. Indoor Air Quality

[An appropriate disclaimer and warning regarding possible indoor air quality problems, including radon, should be inserted here by the builder (see Chapter 3, "Environmental Liability in Real Estate Transactions.")]

I/we acknowledge having read and understood and received a copy of the above outline of nonwarrantable items. We understand and agree that these are conditions for which we have not contracted and will not hold the builder liable.

____________________ (buyer)	____________________ (builder)
____________________ (buyer)	By____________________
Date ____________________	Title____________________
	Date ____________________

6

Inspections

The builder can limit many claims by inspecting the property with the buyer and recording the process. Experience has demonstrated that improved communication lessens the chance that a consumer will file a lawsuit. Many problems arise because buyers have unrealistic expectations or simply do not understand the complexities of the construction process. The construction contract, the limited warranty, statement of nonwarrantable conditions, and all of the other documents involved in the construction process should be designed to explain the process to the buyer in simple and understandable terms. At the same time, these documents may serve as evidence of what actually occurred during the construction process if a dispute should arise.

Home Maintenance Instruction

Before the buyer moves into the new house, the builder or the builder's representative should walk through the house with the buyer and explain what has been done and how the equipment, appliances, and other items work. During this instruction walk-through, the builder should discuss with the buyer the maintenance and the care of items for which the buyer is responsible. Educating the buyer and completing the checklist in Figure 6-1 may prevent problems (a) that result from poor maintenance and (b) that the buyer may try to blame on the builder. At least, the buyer will see and will have in writing the items that are the buyer's responsibility and, thus, may be deterred from trying to blame the builder.

Figure 6-1, "Sample Home Maintenance Checklist," lists the items that should be discussed with the buyer. It also serves as the builder's record of disclosures made to the buyer. This sample does not attempt to include all of the items that should be addressed by the builder. The builder should develop and use a format and list that works best for each particular situation.

Presettlement Walk-Through and the Punchlist

At the same time that the builder demonstrates the various items in the house to the buyer or subsequent to that event, the buyer must inspect the house for defects, problems, or any aspects of construction with which the buyer is dissatisfied. The construction contract should require the buyer to make this inspection before the closing (see Section 2-13, "Inspection, Acceptance, and Possession," in Chapter 2, "Contract between Builder and Buyer or Owner."

As the builder walks through thehouse with the buyer prior to closing, the buyer fills out the punchlist (Figure 6-2, "Sample Punchlist"). The buyer should be required (a) to initial every single item that he/she approves and (b) to specifically identify items that require improvement and spell out what is wrong. These items should be corrected before closing and before the buyer is allowed to move into the house. Special provision should be made for corrections that will require more time (e.g., because of the need to order parts).

The buyer and the builder should agree on a timetable for improvements and write it on the punchlist. They should also set a date, 30 days or so after the closing, for a final inspection so the builder can check on the minor adjustments that were warranted for a 30-day period (e.g., dripping faucets and sticking doors).

In order to avoid the problem of a buyer repeatedly calling a builder to report minor problems in the days or weeks after moving in, the builder might suggest that the buyer keep a record of all minor problems and present it to the builder at one time.

As items on the "Improvement Needed" part of the punchlist are corrected, the buyer should initial and date each item. The builder must keep this punchlist on file until the statute of limitations has expired. If used prop erly, the punchlist is good evidence of the condition of the house and of the buyer's satisfaction with the condition of the house. Used with the limited warranty, the punchlist provides further limitations on a builder's liability if the warranty is designed to exclude liability for damage or defects that the buyer should have discovered and listed for correction during the inspection.

The list may also serve as evidence that, in fact, the buyer was satisfied with the items in the house at one point in time. It also demonstrates the builder's efforts to identify and correct problems.

The punchlist format presented here is merely a suggestion. Different items may apply to other houses, and the builder should consider carefully what format works best in a given situation. The builder could provide a separate punchlist for each room in the house. The list for each room should bear the name of the room to which it applies, and the same format should be used before and after the closing.

Figure 6-1. Sample Home Maintenance Instruction Checklist

Buyer's Name ________________________ Date ________________

Property Address____

Plumbing

1. Instruction on use of faucets (emphasize cleaning of aerator); show water cutoffs; and explain how to change washers, if used. ______
2. Instruction on use of shower and tub drains and care of fiberglass surfaces; show water cutoffs. ______
3. Instruction on adjustment of toilet tank mechanism. ______
4. Explain care of hot water heater ______
   - A. Periodically check pop-off valve and line. ______
   - B. If water is not hot, check the pilot first. ______
   - C. Always turn off pilot (or circuit breaker with electric water heaters) before draining tank completely. ______
   - D. Periodically flush tank. ______
5. Show location of water meter, main cutoff, and sink and sewer cleanouts (in case of an emergency, remove cap and allow sewer to overflow outside). ______
6. Show location of any plumbing access panels and their purpose. ______
7. Show location of well and septic tank, if any; how to care for tank and field; and pumping of tank. Provide instruction on care of well pump. ______

Electrical

8. Show buyer which outlets are switch-controlled. ______
9. Explain correct bulb size for lighting fixtures. ______
10. Show location of main entrance panel. ______
11. Explain circuit breakers and "no fault" circuit breakers and how to operate them. ______
12. Explain operation and testing of smoke detectors. ______
13. Explain operation of security system, intercom, telephone, doorbells, and cable connection for television, if any of these are installed. Show all electrical outlets. ______

Heating and Air-Conditioning

14. Explain warranty. ______
15. Show location and operation of thermostats. ______
16. Show location of filters and explain when they should be changed. ______
17. Explain how to balance forced-air systems in heating and cooling seasons. ______
18. Explain operation of heat pump, if installed, and back-up electric resistance heat. ______
19. Explain operation of hot water heating system and zones or electric baseboard heating, if installed. ______
20. Explain that, if problems with heating or cooling develop, buyer should do the following in the order listed: ______
    - A. Check thermostat setting.
    - B. Check breaker box (be sure breaker is on; explain that breaker switch should be turned all the way off first, then turned back on) ______
    - C. Reset switches ______
21. Furnish name of company to call for service. ______

Figure 6-1. Sample Home Maintenance Instruction Checklist (cont.)

Appliances

22. Instruction on use and care of all appliances. ______
23. Explain limited warranties and give buyer other literature. ______
24. Explain filter and cleaning of range hood. ______
25. Explain how to clean dryer vent pipe and filter. ______
26. Explain that, if appliances do not operate: ______
    - A. Check to be sure they are plugged in. ______
    - B. Check breakers (see item 20). ______
    - C. Reset. ______
27. Furnish name of service company to call for direct service. ______

General Interior

28. Explain care, cleaning, and treatment of floors: wood, carpet, tile. Suggest use of casters under furniture (no warranty for damage caused by neglect). ______
29. Explain care of paint (not warranted) and that builder does not do touch ups). Remind buyer not to scrub latex-painted interior wall. Provide names of paints used and color numbers to buyer. ______
30. Explain use of spackling for normal cracks in sheetrock and nail pops (not warranted). ______
31. Explain use of caulk for cracks in tile and to reseal tub when required (not warranted). ______
32. Explain care of counter tops (Knives will cut the surface.) ______
33. Doors ______
    - A. Clean weep holes in sliding glass door thresholds. ______
    - B. Replace weatherstripping when it wears out or is damaged. ______
    - C. Oil hinges if doors squeak. ______
    - D. Avoid paint buildup on door and window sash edges to keep them from sticking. ______
34. Explain operation of fireplace (if installed), use of seasoned wood to prevent creosote build-up, and the necessity of regularly having flue cleaned. ______
35. Explain types of cleaning products (e.g., nonabrasive materials to be used on counter tops, wood finishes, bathroom tile, fiberglass showers and tubs, porcelain, marble and cultured marble [if used], etc.) ______
36. Explain that bathroom and privacy locks can be unlocked from the outside with small screwdriver or coat hanger. ______
37. Demonstrate removal of window sash for cleaning. ______
38. Explain operation of exterior door and window locks. ______

General Exterior[6-1]

39. Show location of and explain secondary air-conditioning drain. ______
40. Explain hairline expansion cracks in concrete surfaces. ______
41. Explain that sunken utility lines and washed-out areas are not warranted. ______
42. Explain that grass and shrubs are not warranted.(Be certain that grass and shrubs are alive now.) Explain need for fertilizer and plenty of water. ______
43. Light fixtures (bulbs not warranted). ______
44. Explain that hairline cracks in concrete pad and puddles of 1/4 inch are normal. ______
45. Explain that treated lumber used in wood decks, steps, or railings should weather one year prior to staining. ______

[6-1] If builder has installed a radon mitigation system, the builder should include instructions on how to operate it.

Figure 6-1. Sample Home Maintenance Instruction Checklist (cont.)

46. Provide warranties on garage door openers and name of subcontractor. ______
47. Wood siding (if used) must be repainted or stained every 4 to 5 years. Mildew can be removed by scrubbing with weak water-and-bleach solution. Aluminum siding will dent if struck; it can be repainted. Vinyl siding can crack or break if struck. ______
48. Brick ______
49. Roof ______
50. Windows ______
50. Glass ______
46. Other ______

I/We have discussed and understand each of the items listed above with a representative from ________ ______(name of builder)______. I/We have been instructed in the use and care of the above-listed items in my/our new home and find my/our home completed in a manner satisfactory and acceptable to me/us.

______________________ (buyer's signature)   ______________________ (builder)

______________________ (city, state)   By ______________________ (builder's name)

Title______________________

Date______________________

Figure 6-2. Sample Punchlist

[This letter is presented to the buyer along with the checklist at the time of the presettlement walk-through to prepare the punchlist.]

Instructions

______(builder's name)______ is proud to welcome you to your new home. Attached to this letter, you will find a checklist to help you inspect your new home. A separate sheet has been provided for each room and area of construction.

Please go through your new home, room by room, and carefully check to see whether all items are in satisfactory condition. Initial the space provided after you have satisfied yourself that the item's condition meets with your approval. If any repairs or adjustments are needed describe the problem in the "Improvement Needed" column, using the back of the page if necessary. Be sure to write in any additional items that are not listed and describe their condition fully. If a listed item does not apply, put an X in the space for your initials.

Before you occupy your home, we will do our best to bring the items that require improvements up to satisfactory condition, consistent with the standards of construction in ______(city, state)______ and with our builder's limited warranty. You will be required to make a second inspection at that time, and you will have the opportunity to check all the items to make sure they meet with your approval.

Sincerely,

____
(name of builder or builder's representative)

____
(title)

Buyer's Checklist

Date________________

Item	Initials	Improvement Needed
Bathroom		
Vanity	_____	____________
Sink	_____	____________
Medicine cabinet	_____	____________
Bathtub	_____	____________
Shower	_____	____________
Shower curtain bar/door	_____	____________
Toilet	_____	____________
Towel bars	_____	____________
Paper holder	_____	____________
Light fixture (not bulbs)	_____	____________
Baseboard heater or air vent	_____	____________
Floor	_____	____________
Walls	_____	____________
Ceiling	_____	____________
Woodwork	_____	____________
Windows	_____	____________
Doors	_____	____________
Other	_____	____________
Kitchen		
Sink	_____	____________
Burner. unit	_____	____________

Item	Initials	Improvement Needed
Oven, range	_____	____________
Hood and exhaust fan	_____	____________
Appliances	_____	____________
Microwave	_____	____________
Mixer	_____	____________
Dishwasher	_____	____________
Refrigerator	_____	____________
Freezer	_____	____________
Disposal	_____	____________
Trash compacter	_____	____________
Cabinets	_____	____________
Drawers	_____	____________
Countertops	_____	____________
Floor	_____	____________
Walls	_____	____________
Ceiling	_____	____________
Light fixtures (not bulbs)	_____	____________
Windows	_____	____________
Doors	_____	____________
Baseboard heater or air vent		
Other	_____	____________

Figure 6-2. Sample Punchlist (cont.)

Item	Location	Initials	Improvement Needed
Living Room, Dining Room, Den, Family Room, Bedroom[6-2]			
Doors		____	__________
Windows		____	__________
Shades		____	__________
Closets		____	__________
Clothing bar		____	__________
Closet doors		____	__________
Light fixtures (not bulbs)		____	__________
Ceiling fan		____	__________
Floor		____	__________
Walls		____	__________
Ceiling		____	
Baseboard heater or air vent		____	__________
Other		____	__________
General Interior			
Interior doors	______	____	__________
Hardware	______	____	__________
Paneling	______	____	__________
Insulation	______	____	__________
Wallpaper, paint	______	____	__________
Fireplace(s)	______	____	__________
Cabinets, bookcases	______	____	__________
Woodwork	______	____	__________
Tile work	______	____	__________
Hallway			
Closets		____	__________
Walls		____	__________
Floors		____	__________
Ceiling			
Light fixtures (not bulbs)		____	__________
Doors		____	__________
Basement or Utility Room			
Washer		____	__________
Dryer		____	__________
Hot water heater		____	__________
Furnace or Heat Pump		____	__________
Doors		____	__________
Walls		____	__________

Item	Initials	Improvement Needed
Glass	____	__________
Ceilings	____	__________
Other items	____	__________
General Exterior		
Paint	____	__________
Siding, brick	____	__________
Chimney	____	__________
Roof	____	__________
Doors	____	__________
Garage	____	__________
Walkways	____	__________
Balcony	____	__________
Light switches	____	__________
Light fixtures (not bulbs)	____	__________
Outlets	____	__________
Shades	____	__________
Vents (dryer, range hood, bathroom fan)	____	__________
Baseboard heater or air vent	____	__________

I understand each of the items on the preceding pages and have discussed each item with a representative of ______ ______ (builder's name) I have been instructed in the use and care of the items listed on the preceding pages of this punchlist. With the sole exception of the items listed under "Improvement Needs, "I find my new home to be completed in a manner satisfactory and acceptable to me. I understand that, with the exception of those items that I have stated under "Improvement Needed," I am purchasing the house as is, and I understand that the builder makes no other guarantees or warranties other than those that are clearly stated in the contract and the other contract documents.

______________________ (buyer's signature)

______________________ (name of builder)

______________________ (buyer's signature)

By ______________________ (signature)

Date______________________

Title ______________________

[6-2]This section should be duplicated for each individual room.

7

Certificate of Acceptance

This certificate of acceptance must be signed by the buyer upon substantial completion of the home. It is referenced in the contract in Section 2-13, "Inspection, Acceptance, and Possession," in Chapter 2, "Contract Between Builder and Buyer or Owner." The builder may wish to simplify the certificate of acceptance in Figure 7-1 by eliminating or reducing the language in paragraphs 1, 3, 4, and 5, which largely repeat provisions already in Chapter 2.

Figure 7-1. Sample Certificate of Acceptance[7-1]

The buyer certifies that all of the terms and conditions of the contract entered into by the buyer and the builder for ______[construction/purchase]______ the of property at______(address of house)______ have been met, and the buyer and the builder further acknowledge and agree as follows:

1. While the house has generally been constructed according to basic plans and specifications contained in the contract documents, the buyer understands that the house may not correspond in many respects with those plans and specifications because changes may have been made before or during construction. These changes may be attributed to a variety of events, including changes in topography, construction techniques, building codes, the availability of material, or other events.

The buyer understands that the builder is not obligated to furnish any "as built" plans, specifications, or drawings of the house, and the buyer has not relied on any plans or specifications that are on file with any governmental or regulatory authority. The buyer also understands that the house may differ in many respects from the models, drawings, maps, pictures, or other depictions of the house the buyer was shown. The buyer acknowledges that variations may exist in the outside and inside dimensions, configurations, colors, location, general appearance, type or brand of equipment, and other characteristics. The buyer has had ample opportunity to measure the square footage and has done so or elected not to do so. ____/____ (buyer's initials)

2. The buyer has inspected the house and the property on which it is located. The buyer has also delivered to the builder a written list of all of the items that the buyer believes (a) have not been properly constructed or (b) are not in proper condition, and has described the specific problems. Except as noted on the list, the buyer accepts the residence and property as is, and acknowledges that from now on the buyer will have no claim against the builder for any item that was not listed that could have been ascertained or observed during the buyer's inspection. The buyer has no objections relating to color, appearance, type or brand of equipment, dimension or size, location, breakage or cracks, or any other conditions that could have been discovered by the buyer during the inspection.____/____ (buyer's initials)

3. The buyer understands that no warranties are being made by the builder except those appearing in the written limited warranty provided by the builder as part of the contract documents. All statements, representations, promises, or warranties made by the builder or any agent of the builder are superseded by the written limited warranty, and the buyer is not relying on any representations, promises, or warranties except for the written limited warranty that is included by reference in this acceptance document.

The buyer understands that the duration of all implied warranties from the builder, including (but not limited to) the implied warranties of fitness, habitability, and workmanlike construction, have been limited by the builder to one year from the date of sale or the date of occupancy, whichever comes first.[7-2]

[Alternative to 3. The buyer understands that the builder has made no implied warranties whatsoever with respect to the construction of the house itself. The builder disclaims any warranties of habitability, fitness, and workmanship, to the extent allowed by law, and any implied warranty that exists despite this disclaimer is limited in duration to a period of one year.____/____ (buyers' initials)

4. The buyer understands that in exchange for the limited warranty and the other provisions of the contract with the builder the buyer will have no right to recover or receive compensation for any incidental, consequential, secondary, punitive, or special damages, nor any damages for aggravation, pain and suffering, mental anguish, or emotional distress, nor any costs or attorneys' fees. This provision shall be enforceable to the extent allowed by law. (Some states do not allow exclusion or limitation of such damages, so it may not apply.) ____/____ (buyer's initials)

5. The buyer and the builder agree that the claim procedures described in the limited warranty and the arbitration procedures described in the contract shall apply to any claims made by the buyer or the builder and the binding arbitration provisions of the contract shall be the sole available remedy for any unresolved dispute relating to the construction of the house. This provision shall be enforced and followed to the extent allowed by law and if the applicable law prohibits binding arbitration from being the sole available remedy, the buyer and the builder nevertheless agree to submit all claims to arbitration before filing any lawsuit on any claim, and agree that the results of the arbitration proceeding shall be admissible as evidence in a subsequent lawsuit on the same claim.[7-3]]

6. The buyer acknowledges satisfaction with the manner in which the sales transaction was closed and receipt of all financial prorations and adjustments and all closing documents to which the buyer is entitled from the builder.

7. Each provision of this certificate is separate and severable from every other provision, and if any single provision is declared invalid or unenforceable, the buyer and the builder understand that all the other provisions will still be considered valid and enforceable. The buyer and the builder agree that every provision of this certificate will survive the closing of the sales transaction and will not be merged with the deed.

__________ (buyer's signature)	__________ (name of builder)
__________ (buyer's signature)	By __________ (signature)
Date__________	Title__________
Date__________	

7-1. Sample language that appears in brackets presents an option for the reader. Depending on the particular transaction the reader must choose one or the other, both, or neither of the possible wordings presented.

7-2. Builders should make sure that this limitation of the implied warranties conforms to any limitation appearing in the limited warranty, see "Limited Warranty," in Chapter 5, "Warranties and Disclaimers," and Section 2-16, "Representations and Warranty," of Chapter 2, "Contract Between Builder and Buyer or Owner."

7-3. Builder should be sure to coordinate this provision with Section 2-11, "Arbitration," Chapter 2, "Contract Between the Builder and the Buyer or Owner."

8

Contract Between Builder and Subcontractor

In addition to the contract with the buyer, contracts with subcontractors can have substantial impact on the liability of all parties. To protect the builder, contracts with subcontractors should clearly delineate the obligations of the subcontractors. For example, such a contract should require that the subcontractor (a) pay all taxes associated with the subcontractor's work and (b) insure the work against fire, other enumerated casualty losses, or "any cause whatsoever." The provision should state that the builder is not under any circumstances accountable to the subcontractor for such losses. Builders should require certificates of liability insurance from subcontractors.

The contract should hold the subcontractor liable for any loss or damage the subcontractor causes on the job site, even if the subcontractor's particular work may have been completed by the time the damage is discovered. In addition, the contract should require the subcontractor to indemnify the builder for all losses, damages, or problems relating to the work undertaken by the subcontractor. This provision helps to protect the builder from actions brought by the buyer or third parties relating to the subcontractor's work.

A conduit clause can pass the builder' obligations to the buyer on to the subcontractor. This provision should state that the builder has the same rights and privileges against the subcontractor as the construction contract gives to the buyer against the builder.

In another provision the subcontractor should acknowledge that the subcontractor (a) has read and understood the construction contract between the builder and buyer or owner and all the plans and specifications and (b) agrees to comply with and perform all of the provisions in those documents that are applicable to the subcontractor.

The provisions listed here illustrate clauses that may be used in construction contracts between builders and subcontractors. These provisions do not address every contingency, nor do they apply to all contracts with subcontractors. Some important provisions are not included here, such as (a) requiring subcontractors to sign lien waivers when they are paid by the builder and (b) requiring subcontractors to acknowledge that they are not authorized to make any representations, promises, or warranties to the home buyer without written prior authorization of the builder. These and other provisions are necessary to protect the builder in particular situations. Thus, builders must carefully consider the facts of each situation and use a contract specifically designed to fit those facts. Because contracts are legal documents that have great impact on builders' liability, they should have their attorneys prepare or, at least, review such documents before signing them.

8-1. Subcontractor Proposal

Comments

The proposal is usually the blueprint for the offer to enter into a contract. The proposal's description of the scope of the work should be precise. The description should state the plans and specifications by page numbers, date of last revisions, and addenda.

When the subcontractor's proposal is signed by the builder, it becomes a binding contract, or the terms and conditions of the proposal may be incorporated into any contract that is subsequently signed by adding the words: "The scope of the work and terms and conditions as stated in __(subcontractor's)__ proposal (dated the __________ day of__________ 19___), are incorporated by reference, and shall take precedence over any conflicting provisions in the contract." Of course, the language of this or any other contract provision can be changed according to the wishes and bargaining strength of the various parties (see sample language in Figure 8-1).

Figure 8-1. Sample Proposal

For: Date________________

________________ Project________________
(name of builder)

________________ Location ________________
(street address)

________________ ________________
(city, state, zip)

Phone ( )________ Design Professional ________
Drawings No.___ Dated ______
Specifications Dated ________

Subject to prompt acceptance within ________ days and to all conditions stipulated below, we propose to furnish materials and labor at the prices as stipulated below:

Price: $ ________

The undersigned accepts this proposal and all its terms and conditions as a binding contract subject only to the approval of the credit of the builder by the subcontractor, which shall not be unreasonably withheld.

________________ (builder)	________________ (subcontractor)
By ________________ (signature)	By ________________ (signature)
Title ________________	Title________________
Date ________________	Date________________

8-2. Payment Terms

The two payment provisions below are alternatives. A builder would prefer the "Contingent Payment" clause while a subcontractor would prefer the "Savings" clause.

Option 1—Contingent Payment

Comments

A typical contingent payment clause follows this paragraph. A number of courts have interpreted payment clauses to allow recovery by subcontractors even though the general contractor is not paid by the buyer. To avoid these rulings, the "conditions precedent" language below is necessary.

Sample Language

The builder agrees to pay the subcontractor within thirty (30) days after the completion of the work, certification by the architect, and payment by the buyer for such work, all of which shall operate as conditions precedent to the builder's obligation to pay the subcontractor.

Option 2—Savings

Comments

A savings clause establishes that the subcontractor will be paid if the builder is not paid by the buyer or if the architect does not certify the work for any reason not the fault of the subcontractor.

Requesting payment 30 days after the completion of the subcontractor's work insures that the subcontractor will not have to wait for the completion of the entire project for compensation. The subcontractor's warranty should be adequate to protect the builder against problems that might arise after the completion of the subcontractor's work.

Sample Language

The builder shall pay the subcontractor for the work and materials supplied by the subcontractor as far as executed and fixed in place, less the retained percentage, within thirty (30) days after completion of the work by the subcontractor if the architect or buyer's authorized agent fails to issue a certification of completion for any reason that is not the fault of the subcontractor.

8-3. The Scope of the Work

Comments

The clause describing the work to be performed in a contract between a builder and a subcontractor must be precise. Otherwise, the subcontractor may be required to perform work not contemplated when bidding on the job or negotiating the contract, or the subcontractor may not perform work that the builder expected to be done.

Dragnet clauses should be avoided in contracts between builders and subcontractors. These clauses provide that subcontractors will perform the usual work of their trades regardless of where the specifications may appear and regardless of the drawings in which the work may appear.

Sample Language

The subcontractor shall furnish the labor, materials, equipment, and supervision necessary to construct or perform the __________ work shown on drawing number ______ through _______ dated ____(date)____, and last revised __________ in accordance with Specification sections ________, dated __________[and excluding the following:]

8-4. Changes

Comments

The changes clause offers protection to the builder, as well as tying the subcontractor into the contract between the builder and the buyer or owner. The builder must retain the right to order changes, in writing, even when terms have not been agreed upon. The builder should have a mechanism to establish a dollar ceiling and other limits in future changes.

Sample Language

The builder may order changes in the work. The subcontractor shall not be entitled to nor shall it receive any increase or upward adjustment in its contract price unless the amount and the liability of the change are acknowledged in writing by the builder and the subcontractor. Otherwise the subcontractor proceeds at its own risk and expense. No alteration, addition, omission, or change shall be made in the work nor in the method or manner of the performance, except upon the written change order of the builder. Any change or adjustment in the contract price by virtue of the change order shall be specifically stated in the change order. No change order shall vary, abrogate, avoid, or otherwise affect the terms, conditions, and provisions of this contract except as specifically stated in the change order.

8-5. Insurance and Indemnification

Comments

The subcontractor should have direct liability for its acts or the acts of its employees and agents. As an alternative to the sample language below, the hold-harmless and indemnity clauses, as well as insurance requirements, in a contract may be limited strictly to injuries and to damages caused by the negligence of the subcontractor or the subcontractor's agents and employees.

Sample Language

The builder shall not be liable for any loss or casualty incurred or caused by the subcontractor. The subcontractor shall maintain at the subcontractor's own expense full and complete insurance on its work until final acceptance of the work on the contract between the builder and the buyer or owner. The builder is not responsible for providing any protective service for the subcontractor's benefit and is not liable for any loss or damage to the subcontractor's work or equipment.

The subcontractor shall hold the builder harmless from any and all liability, costs, damages, attorney's fees, and expenses from any claims or causes of action arising while on or near the project, or while performing contract-related work, including those claims relating to the subcontractor's subcontractors, suppliers, or employees, or by reason of any claim or dispute of any person or entity for damages from any cause directly or indirectly relating to any action or failure to act by the subcontractor, its representatives, employees, subcontractors, or suppliers. The builder may retain any and all monies due or to become due to the subcontractor under this or any other contract, sufficient to save itself harmless and indemnify itself against any liability or damage, including attorney's fees. Failure of the subcontractor to maintain complete insurance may be deemed a material breach allowing the builder to terminate this contract or to provide insurance at the subcontractor's sole expense. In neither case, however, shall the subcontractor's liability be lessened.

8-6. Taxes, Charges, and Permits

Comments

This clause makes the subcontractor responsible for the taxes, fees, and other charges generated by the subcontractor's work under the contract. This clause also holds the subcontractor accountable for securing the necessary permits for completing its portion of the project.

Sample Language

The subcontractor understands and agrees that it is an independent contractor, and that it shall be responsible for and pay any and all taxes, contributions, fees, and similar expenses imposed directly or indirectly for its work, labor, material, and services required by or relating to this contract. The subcontractor shall at the subcontractor's own expense apply for and obtain all necessary permits and conform strictly to the laws, ordinances, and regulations applicable in the locality where the work is performed. At no time shall the contract price increase or escalate on account of any such charge. On demand, the subcontractor shall substantiate that all taxes and other charges are being properly paid.

8-7. Cleanup

Comments

The subcontractor should have the responsibility for removal of the debris generated by its work on the job site. The builder should be reimbursed for cleanup if the subcontractor fails to comply with this requirement.

Sample Language

The subcontractor shall at all times keep the building and premises clean of dirt, debris, rubbish, and any other waste materials arising from the performance of this subcontract. The subcontractor is responsible for the removal and disposal of all receptacles and containers in which these materials are deposited. On the completion of the portions of its work, the subcontractor shall broom clean its work areas. The subcontractor shall perform whatever additional cleanup work that is directed by the builder at no additional cost to the builder. If waste from this subcontractor is found on the job, the builder shall be compensated for the cost of removing the subcontractor's trash and shall be entitled to deduct the costs thereof from any monies owed to the subcontractor.

8-8. Liquidated Damages

Comments

This clause provides for liquidated damages caused by delay. Liquidated damages are not a penalty to be inflicted on the subcontractor. Therefore, the amount of liquidated damages must bear an actual or reasonably estimated relationship to the actual losses the builder will suffer if the project is not completed on time.

As in the builder's contract with the buyer, the contract with the subcontractor may also include a bonus provision to offset the liquidated damages clause.

Sample Language

If the project is not substantially completed on the completion date set by this contract, the subcontractor (or the subcontractor's surety) shall pay to the builder the sum of $________ for each calendar day of inexcusable delay until the work is substantially completed, as liquidated damages.

The subcontractor will use its best efforts to complete its work prior to the completion date. However, if the subcontractor is delayed at any time in the progress of its work for reasons beyond its control, such as the unavailability of materials, inclement weather, strikes, changes in governmental regulations, acts of governmental agencies or their employees, acts of God, or the failure of the architect, buyer, or builder to cooperate, or because of any other reason beyond the control of the subcontractor, the builder will extend the date of completion for a period equal to the time of the delays.

Learn More About Business Practices for Builders and Remodelers from These Home Builder Press Books

Accounting and Financial Management

Focuses on job cost control methods. Includes information on designing an accounting system, choosing an accountant, terminology and procedures, and planning and analysis. Reflects the 1986 tax law changes and features a chapter specifically for accountants. The NAHB Chart of Accounts includes job cost control, subsidiary ledger accounts for direct, indirect, and land development costs. 2nd ed., 1988, 96 pp. ISBN 0-86718-319-5

Computer Handbook for Builders

Computers can save time and money—and increase productivity. This *Handbook* helps you evaluate and choose the right system for your accounting, estimating, and office work. Clear, easy-to-understand descriptions help you ask the right questions to find the ideal system. Features useful checklists and a glossary of common terms. 1989, 137 pp. ISBN 0-86718-326-8

Remodelers Business Basics

Provides a hands-on approach to running a remodeling company. Author Linda W. Case (a successful remodeler herself) tells remodelers and specialty and single-line contractors how to survive the first 5 years of business—when the failure rate is high. Covers financial management, marketing, production, insurance, and more. An invaluable resource for seasoned remodelers and builders who are diversifying. Includes sample contract clauses, bibliography, and over 90 forms, checklists, and guidelines. 1988, 232 pp. ISBN 0-86718-300-4

Additional books are available from the Home Builder Bookstore. To place an order or obtain a catalog, write or call:

Home Builder Bookstore
National Association of Home Builders
15th and M Streets, N.W.
Washington, D.C. 20005
(800) 368-5242 Ext. 463

AF708474

THE SINGING SCULPTURE. Photographed by Lord Snowdon
for *The Sunday Times Magazine*, London, January 10, 1971.

GILBERT & GEORGE

BRENDA RICHARDSON

THE BALTIMORE MUSEUM OF ART

DATES OF THE EXHIBITION

THE BALTIMORE MUSEUM OF ART
February 19–April 15, 1984

CONTEMPORARY ARTS MUSEUM, HOUSTON
June 23–August 19, 1984

THE NORTON GALLERY OF ART, WEST PALM BEACH, FLORIDA
September 29–November 25, 1984

MILWAUKEE ART MUSEUM, MILWAUKEE, WISCONSIN
January 11–March 17, 1985

THE SOLOMON R. GUGGENHEIM MUSEUM, NEW YORK
April 26–June 16, 1985

FOREWORD

It is a special privilege to introduce *Gilbert & George*, a book published in conjunction with one of the most exciting contemporary art exhibitions ever sponsored by The Baltimore Museum of Art. This much-anticipated exhibition and its accompanying publication comprise the first substantive examination in America of the work of these two prominent and influential English artists. Since 1967, when they met and formed their artistic collaboration, Gilbert and George have created an exceptional body of work in a wide range of mediums and genres. They have been so prolific that a comprehensive retrospective of all of the forms in which they have worked is unrealistic. Accordingly, the Baltimore project consists of a full-scale retrospective of their "photo-pieces," a form they invented in 1971 and in which they have worked consistently to the present day.

The art of Gilbert and George is unique in form and daring in subject matter. It is controversial, often seemingly enigmatic work, and has been subject over the years to frequent misinterpretation by critics and public alike. It is our hope that this broad overview of the artists' photo-pieces will provide viewers with the opportunity for a clearer, more revelatory understanding of the work of Gilbert and George.

To the Board of Trustees of The Baltimore Museum of Art, I want to express our warmest gratitude for its enthusiastic support of this ambitious endeavor. Several Board members have been especially encouraging in their commitment to the Museum's programs in contemporary art, but the Board as a whole has never wavered in its devotion to curatorial decisions regarding exhibition programming, no matter how progressive. It is an honor to work with such a dedicated and enlightened group of individuals.

In turn, and on behalf of the entire Board of Trustees, I wish to extend our deepest respect and appreciation to Brenda Richardson, the Museum's Assistant Director for Art and Curator of Painting and Sculpture, who conceived of the exhibition in 1978 and dedicated herself to bringing the art of Gilbert and George to a wider American audience in the most comprehensive and enlightening manner possible. Her commitment to the artists' work has sustained her through almost three years of complex, often difficult organizational efforts to bring the project to fruition. There are no words sufficient to express our admiration for her accomplishment.

Gilbert & George represents a project of international scope and considerable financial obligation to the Museum. Accordingly, it is with the most profound gratitude that I am able to acknowledge the crucial role of the exhibition's national corporate sponsor, Best Products Co., Inc., in making it possible for the Museum to support both the exhibition and its catalogue at optimum scope and quality. There is no precedent in the often-controversial arena of modern art exhibitions for the magnitude of generosity manifest by Best Products Co., Inc. in assuming full corporate sponsorship for *Gilbert & George*. It is an honor to pay tribute in this regard to the farsighted leadership of Best's Chairman and Chief Executive Officer, Sydney Lewis, and to Frances A. Lewis, Executive Vice President. Mr. and Mrs. Lewis have demonstrated their commitment to contemporary art in countless ways over several decades, but never more meaningfully than in their generous support to this important project. We are equally grateful to Susan L. Butler, Director of the Best Products Foundation, who took an active interest in the Gilbert & George exhibition from the time of its inception. We are confident that it was through Mrs. Butler's personal conviction that we are today in a position to extend our thanks to the entire Board of the Best Products Foundation for its support and major financial subsidy. Edwin Slipek, Assistant

Vice President of Best Products Co., Inc., coordinated all of the public relations aspects of the collaboration between the Museum and Best Products. His enthusiasm for the exhibition and his interest in working closely with all of the museums on the show's national circulation to assure the widest possible audience for the artists' work have been extraordinarily gratifying.

We are equally grateful to several other sources of support for the exhibition. The National Endowment for the Arts, Washington, D.C., provided a generous grant to the exhibition and publication, and I want to thank both its Chairman, Frank S. M. Hodsoll, and its Museum Program Director, Andrew Oliver, for their assistance. The British Council also extended a grant in support of this important exhibition of contemporary English art. In particular, we are eager to note the active involvement of Julian Andrews, Director of the Fine Arts Department of The British Council in London, whose personal interest in the work of Gilbert and George resulted in persistent efforts to find funding assistance for the project, and to Hugh R. Crooke, Cultural Attaché of the British Embassy in Washington, and Mrs. Sally de Sousa, his assistant, both of whom extended enthusiastic support for the Museum's organization of *Gilbert & George*. Additional support was generously provided by the artists' primary gallery representatives, the Anthony d'Offay Gallery in London, and the Sonnabend Gallery in New York City.

We are extremely pleased by the prestigious national circulation of the Gilbert & George exhibition, and I want to extend my thanks to my colleague museum directors who shared our commitment to this art: Linda L. Cathcart of the Contemporary Arts Museum, Houston; Richard A. Madigan of The Norton Gallery of Art, West Palm Beach, Florida; Gerald Nordland of the Milwaukee Art Museum; and Diane Waldman of The Solomon R. Guggenheim Museum, New York. They and their respective staff members have shown genuine dedication and extraordinary professionalism in mounting this complex exhibition.

The Gilbert & George exhibition represents as complicated and difficult an organizational assignment as can be imagined. The project could not have been managed effectively without the personal attention of many people both here and abroad. In London, in particular, the staff of the Anthony d'Offay Gallery assumed the role of virtual collaborators, offering day to day technical and administrative assistance to Brenda Richardson from the earliest stages of the exhibition's organization. Anne and Anthony d'Offay have given their constant attention to the project, extending countless courtesies over the past two years and providing essential support in every way; on the d'Offay staff, Judy Adam, Marie-Louise Laband, and Raymond Webb have offered their fullest cooperation, becoming virtual extensions of the Baltimore Museum staff in bringing the project to successful completion. In New York, Ileana Sonnabend responded to Brenda's initial exhibition proposal in 1978 with a degree of support that went far beyond her role as the artists' American dealer. Mrs. Sonnabend's friendship has been a constant source of encouragement and a vital impetus to the project. Antonio Homem, Director of the Sonnabend Gallery, and Nick Sheidy of the gallery's staff have been of invaluable assistance. The artists' gallery representatives in Paris and Amsterdam have also been of enormous aid in coordinating the shipment of works from France and Holland. We would like to thank Chantal Crousel and Ghislaine Hussenot of the Galerie Crousel-Hussenot in Paris, and Adriaan van Ravesteijn of Art & Project, Amsterdam, for their cooperation.

The many lenders, both public and private, who agreed to permit their Gilbert and George photo-pieces to be included in this exhibition, deserve our special acknowledgment. Works have been borrowed from all over the world, in many instances from public institutions where those works form an essential part of permanent collection displays, or from private homes where these works are the centerpieces of a personal environment. The collectors of Gilbert and George comprise a unique group of individuals, with an unusually passionate commitment to the work. We know it is a hardship for them to be separated from their photo-pieces for such an extended period of time, and we are very grateful for their generosity in sharing these works with a wider public.

The primary organizational burden of the show, of course, falls to the staff of The Baltimore Museum of Art. As always, our Museum family has lent its most concerted efforts toward assuring the safe and successful conclusion of this exhibition activity. On behalf of Brenda Richardson, I especially want to note the active role of William C. Ameringer, Assistant Curator of Painting and Sculpture, who provided day to day assistance throughout the project's organizational stages. L. Carol Murray, Senior Registrar, coordinated the unusually complex and delicate handling and shipping arrangements, as well as managing the physical security of the works throughout their American tour. Karen E. Nielsen organized and supervised the installation team in charge of mounting the exhibition's almost 1,500 units both in Baltimore and at each of its circulation venues. Audrey Frantz coordinated all phases of the publication, bringing her impressive administrative skills to bear on an unusually challenging production assignment. The book itself, beautifully designed by Gilbert and George with the sensitive collaboration of the Museum's graphic artists, Alex and Caroline Castro of Baltimore, is a tribute to the loving involvement of everyone involved with its production. Extraordinary efforts were made to assure the highest publication quality, including seven-color press work to guarantee fidelity in the book's lavish illustrations. In this regard, it is with special appreciation that we note the commitment of Michael Feeney of Schneidereith & Sons, Baltimore, printers of the book, and David Rosquist of Prolith International, Inc., Beltsville, Maryland, who supervised the technical aspects of producing the book's eighty-one full-color illustrations.

In the course of preparing the book's perceptive text, Brenda Richardson had the moral support and practical encouragement of several friends and colleagues in particular. Ann Allston Boyce, the Museum's Assistant Director for Administration, edited the manuscript and offered daily research assistance and enthusiastic interest. Carol Lindsley and Dr. Gertrude Rosenthal both read the manuscript at each of its three draft stages and offered insightful and constructive criticisms. Brenda Richardson is, however, her own severest critic, and the brilliant text published to accompany this exhibition stands as the definitive writing on the work of Gilbert and George to date.

Finally, on behalf of Brenda and myself, as well as the Board of Trustees, I want to express our warmest thanks to Gilbert and George, the "living sculpture," who extended their confidence in The Baltimore Museum of Art by granting the necessary cooperation to mount this first American retrospective of their work. The artists have been an integral part of every aspect of the exhibition and publication organization and have demonstrated a remarkable degree of stamina and involvement in giving freely of their time, their thoughts and feelings, their creative energies, and their organizational skills, as well as permitting full access to their documentary and photographic archives. Working in the closest possible collaboration with Brenda Richardson, the artists designed not only the book but also the unique installation of the exhibition at each of its venues. Their commitment to the project will endure through all of the exhibition's circulation, as they work side by side with the Museum's own staff in hanging the shows in Baltimore, Houston, West Palm Beach, Milwaukee, and New York. We are deeply indebted to Gilbert and George for their friendship and for the sincere dedication they brought to this exhibition proposal, as well as for the impressive and moving body of work around which the exhibition is built.

Arnold L. Lehman
Director

GILBERT & GEORGE

"no puzzle, just difficult truth"

Gilbert and George are two persons and one artist at the same time. They have constructed a persona marked with paradox and poetry, and sculpted it with such carefully delineated form that they and their work seem to grow ever more enigmatic and, to some, impenetrable. The artists consider the mystique and mystery surrounding their passage through life as "living sculpture" (fig. 1) to be of essential importance to the meaning of their work and thus resist both biographical and traditional art historical explication as being potentially damaging to the individual's personal interpretive experience of their art. For Gilbert and George art is not simply a vocation, and it is totally characteristic that they would wish to shroud their lives and their working methods, as well as the iconographical and even metaphorical content of the work, in a veil of bombast and contradiction. Art for Gilbert and George is a passion and a religion, and for them art-being gradually subsumed the more typical evolution of human behavior. Step by step, year by year, they cast all personal actions and all manner of social intercourse in the form of "living sculpture":

> We are only human sculptors in that we get up every day, walking sometimes, reading rarely, eating often, thinking always, smoking moderately, enjoying enjoyment, looking, relaxing to see, loving nightly, finding amusement, encouraging life, fighting boredom, being natural, daydreaming, travelling along, drawing occasionally, talking lightly, tea drinking, feeling tired, dancing sometimes, philosophising a lot, criticising never, whistling tunefully, dying very slowly, laughing nervously, greeting politely and waiting till the day breaks.[1]

Gilbert and George met and formed their artistic collaboration in 1967, when they were both students at St. Martin's School of Art in London (fig. 2). Gilbert was born in 1943 in the Alpine region of northeastern Italy, the Dolomites, and George was born in 1942 in a small town in Devon, England. They live an orderly and comfortable (though somewhat monastic) life in a renovated eighteenth-century rowhouse on Fournier Street near Spitalfields, a working class London neighborhood; they maintain family and religious ties; they socialize with a small circle of friends; they are passionate collectors of the furniture and pottery of the English Neo-Gothic and Arts & Crafts movements, and they live midst this shared world of extraordinary objects with reverence and awe (fig. 3). Their decision to become "living sculpture" derived from a need to devote their lives to art. They approached such a prospect as if they were entering a religious order and accordingly created a life in which mundane details require virtually no deliberation and suffer little alteration from day to day. For the sake of simplicity and convenience, most days they eat breakfast, lunch, and dinner at the same neighborhood workman's cafe, which they treat as an extension of their home. In order to eliminate issues of choice and vanity, they adopted a uniform (what they call "the responsibility-suits of our art") comprised of white nylon shirts (George's cuff-linked and Gilbert's button-cuffed), loud or often emblematic ties, and worsted suits. Although they often travel in conjunction with their exhibition projects, they have no automobile and take no holidays. By adopting such an unorthodox lifestyle, they are able to reserve their decision-making energy almost entirely for their art work. They consciously endeavor to reduce conflict in their lives, and even more consciously aspire toward what they call "being well-behaved," an aspiration which, in its broadest interpre-

Fig. 1. THE RED SCULPTURE (Detail of ''Ready'' Section), 1975.

Fig. 2. GILBERT AND GEORGE AT ST. MARTIN'S, Spring 1968.

Fig. 4. "ARTIST'S CULTURE" (Detail of Cover), from *The Limericks*, Postal Sculpture, Spring 1971.

Fig. 3. INTERIOR OF THE ARTISTS' HOUSE, November 1983.

tation, comprises their personal moral code. They firmly believe that fairness is important and they try not to be destructive. They assume a sanguine attitude toward the world, a consuming philosophy expressed with equal intensity in their life and work. They believe that art is dealing with the whole of life, from horror to ecstasy, from prehistoric past to present, excluding nothing. This principle of acceptance of the whole, acted out in every aspect of life, produces the appearance of a striking composure on the part of both men. It is this unusual degree of composure, broken only under stress, that lends definition and credibility to the "living sculpture."

As "living sculpture," Gilbert and George are very much an indivisible unit. That they are so universally accepted as one is a tribute to the merging of their minds and spirits, since as individuals they are quite distinct: George is tall and fair, Gilbert is shorter and dark; George wears glasses, Gilbert does not; George smokes heavily, Gilbert does not smoke at all; George is a Methodist, Gilbert is a Catholic. They are correctly polite to each other at all times; they never interrupt one another, though they often finish each other's paragraphs at alternating sentence pauses; neither is observedly subservient to the other. They share equally in the art-making; they can each perform every aspect of the art production competently. They work on the same drawings jointly; it is impossible to ascertain uniquely distinguishing features of the hand of either in any given work. They conceptualize in tandem and claim never to reach widely divergent creative resolutions. Each offers constant constructive support to the other. Negative criticism is gently proffered and instantly withdrawn if offense is taken. They like and respect each other and demonstrate a palpable degree of tenderness and concern for one another's well-being and individual ego. They offer one another freedom of self. They are never lonely.

In a 1971 postal sculpture, *The Limericks*, an eight-part series of printed limericks mailed to selected recipients at the rate of one per week for eight weeks, they included the piece called "Artist's Culture" (fig. 4):

> There were two young men who were charming as sweets
> They turned the heads of all in the streets
> They looked at their ties and laughed and were pleased
> Looking down to their socks they began to sneeze
> The boys didn't mind as much as they might
> For they were artists and that was their plight
> The funny thing is they're really quite normal
> It's just that they seem of another order.

Like most of their pronouncements, issued in the form of poetry or lyrical prose and often published by the artists in beautifully designed, limited-edition, hand-printed books, this one too is conceived to perpetuate their fictive persona. For of course they are not at all "really quite normal" and they are indeed "of another order." With each year since the invention of the "living sculpture," Gilbert and George have gotten a firmer grasp on the details of their sculptural image, and it becomes ever more elaborate. They have attained a granitic, intractable conviction about who they are and what they believe, and they have contained and routinized their life patterns to express that conviction. Despite how thoroughly identity-specific their pose has become over the course of fifteen years, there remains an evident self-consciousness in the constant effort to sustain the image reflected with such frozen permanence in the work. They move through life in the same uniforms which have become so familiar from the self-portraits that recur in the photo-pieces, and they project into the world an impression of theatricality which can be frightening in its consistency. There is in the public apprehension of the persona only the most negligible of distinctions between life and art as conducted by Gilbert and George.

"the most serious intentions in the world"

In 1969 the artists compiled what they call their "Life Box," a box filled with images, writings, and small objects descriptive of their work, and "strode out into the art world." They made appointments to visit dealers, critics, museum curators, and anyone else associated with the broader English art world, in order to expand awareness of their presence in that world. They often kept their appointments with their foreheads spray-painted with their *Design for Foreheads*, a logo composed of the letters G and G and handsome self-likenesses (George wore Gilbert's image, and Gilbert wore George's [fig. 5]). Reflecting on this now, both men chuckle appreciatively at the daring confidence with which they approached these potentially vital encounters.

Within the London art world by this time, Gilbert and George were already a known quantity. Although reviews, both then and now, often link them to the history of "performance art," at least in London by 1970 they

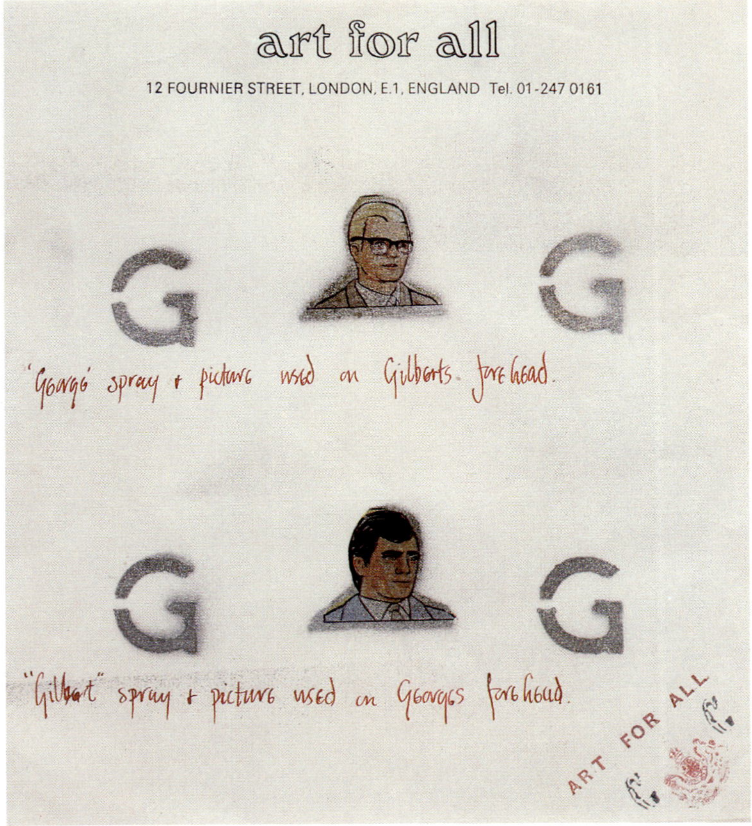

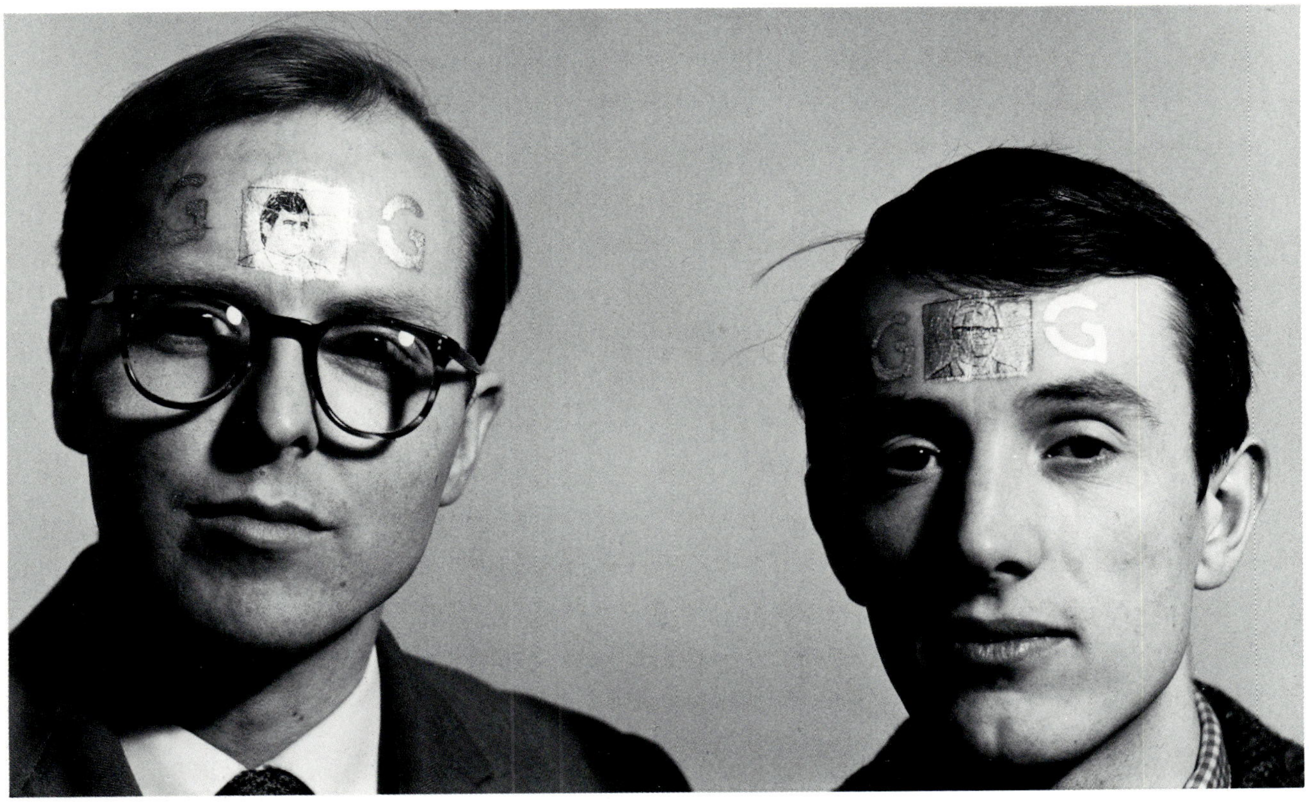

Fig. 5. DESIGN FOR FOREHEADS, 1969.

Fig. 6. THE SINGING SCULPTURE.

May we describe to you with picture and words a sculpture which began on the last Saterday in November of '69 we had just made some cocoa when it began to snow so we positioned ourselves at the window as we began to look we felt ourselves taken into a sculpture of overwhelming purity life and peace a rare and new art-piece we thank you for being with us for these few moments

Yours sincerely Gilbert *and* George

'Art for All,' 12 Fournier Street, London, E.1, England

Fig. 7. "MAY WE DESCRIBE TO YOU," Postal Sculpture, November 1969.

Fig. 8. MAGAZINE SCULPTURE, 1969.

were widely accepted and identified as "living sculpture" (fig. 6). The context and audience may vary, but Gilbert and George steadfastly maintain their pose in public and private. As such, they have always considered their scheduled public presentations simply an extension of their lifestyle as "living sculpture," rather than a discrete work of art or "performance." From their earliest formal exhibitions, they set the tone of how they wished the work to be received: with dignity, respect, decorum, and seriousness. In the spring of 1968 they issued engraved invitations to their exhibition, *Three Works/Three Works*, at Frank's Sandwich Bar on Silver Place in London. The exhibition was comprised of "object-sculptures" made by Gilbert and George and arranged tastefully on the cloth-covered cafe tables, with guests invited for a two-hour period. This earliest printed invitation, in classic "wedding script," incorporated the logo of "G.P." and "G.P.," the artists' shared initials (it wasn't until mid-1969 that they dropped the surname initial from their logo and became just Gilbert and George). Formality and proper etiquette have indelibly marked the public face of their work from the earliest moment of their collaboration. They are obsessed with manners, and their controlled deportment and fastidiousness of detail were integrated into the work as aesthetic content.

Initially, the form of the work was determined rather pragmatically. They opposed the concept of the art object as consumer merchandise and sought an alternative to the established art market system. They were determined to abandon physical object sculpture and, in any case, once out of school they had no studio and no money to buy materials. Since they had only themselves, they became their own sculpture as an economical and incorrupt means of expressing their art ideas. When objects appeared in the work, they were street debris or cheap found materials (food, plaster cake decorations, postcards) or nature (snow, tree branches and foliage, flowers, sunlight through windows [fig. 7]). The art form devised by Gilbert and George was both original and exceedingly radical for its time. They grew up as artists in the mid- to late 1960's under the domination of Pop Art and Minimalism, movements given to non-judgmental content and anti-expressionist form. Gilbert and George, quite contrarily, were committed to meaning and morality in art and to imaginative expressionism as the most honest and direct form of communication. When they decided to use their own bodies as art material and their personal convictions as content, they literally invented their own medium and carved out a unique and memorable place for themselves in the evolution of contemporary art.

Although Gilbert and George did not set out to create art that would shock their public, they were aware of the importance to them of expressing extreme states of consciousness. In about 1970 they remarked to their closest friend (and later English representative), London art dealer Anthony d'Offay, "We always feel that our art has a great deal to do with embarrassment." Gilbert confesses, for instance, that to this day he is still embarrassed by their 1969–1970 *Magazine Sculpture*, photo-portraits in which the artists appear with cut-out letters pinned to their ties and suit-fronts, spelling "George the Cunt" and "Gilbert the Shit" (fig. 8). They made a conscious decision to address in their art all of the concerns that envelop our lives, even and especially those concerns that most people deem "private." In this respect, they often select subject matter that in previous times would have been considered inappropriate or even indecent for fine art. Gilbert and George's subjects may be shocking only by virtue of their unfamiliarity as art content. "We want to *un-shock* people," they report, "and bringing these subjects into the open, allowing them to live and breathe, should un-shock." While even the artists describe some of their works as "dirty" or "naughty" or "rude," their art is never pornographic—it is designed to evoke a strong reaction in the viewer, not to elicit prurient interest. There is nothing in the work of Gilbert and George that is not a universal of everyone's public or private experience: sex, religion, socioeconomic deprivation, government, urban development, nature, misery, ecstasy, human interaction, death. Unlike most of us, however, Gilbert and George have the courage to embarrass themselves, if need be, by articulating both "good" and "bad" thoughts and "good" and "bad" living in a public medium. The artists address these subjects from a personal and experiential, though not strictly autobiographical, perspective. Their portraits are often injected into the work's narrative, and indeed frequently seem to be the primary subject. Their omnipresent self-images, however, are not necessarily to suggest the literal role of Gilbert and George in the specific setting depicted. As symbolic images, they become Everyman—pilgrim, guide, and alter ego for their fellows. This is their uniqueness. They call themselves "campaigning artists" and their work is essentially polemical. Through their work they are quite literally proselytizers for their particular world view, which is

Fig. 9. "CRUSADE," Exhibition of Postcard Sculptures, Installation View, Anthony d'Offay Gallery, London, January 13–February 13, 1982.

Fig. 10. YOUNG SAINT. 1982. Photo-piece, 20-part. 95 × 98¾ in. (242 × 251 cm.). Private Collection, Atlanta.

Fig. 11. LIVING SCULPTURE WITH HEADS, 1969.

their religion (fig. 9). It is one of the many challenging contradictions of this work that the artists who explore such unorthodox and controversial subject matter are, on one level at least, shy, retiring, middle-aged gentlemen in English wools.

The work depicts the world that Gilbert and George see, and sometimes the world they want, and it often intersects the world as they live it. The images used in the work—often "discovered" and captured by the artists in the course of their purposeful wanderings around London—derive very much from personal experience, just as the metaphysical content of the work (its message) reflects their most private and passionate moral convictions. It is possible to trace quite accurately the year-by-year evolution of the work's meaning by looking carefully at the emotional and philosophical development of Gilbert and George in the same years, and vice versa. While much of the iconography is English in source, there is no specificity of sociopolitical intent. The artists live and work in London and draw their resource material from what is familiar and proximate. Like their self-images, other subjects are conceived in broad symbolic terms: London's Houses of Parliament stand for all forms of governmental authority; high-rise office buildings are universal in character and meaning; street tramps are an international urban phenomenon. Such subjects have no restrictively nationalistic association for the artists, and should convey none to the viewer.

The most consistent themes of Gilbert and George's work over the past decade are sex and religion. For the artists, sex is a subject of powerful centrality. They see sex as the single most driving force in life, whether it is the sex of flowers, animals, or humans. They choose to confront boldly in their work the subject that they believe most absorbs most people most of the time and yet, contradictorily, is least addressed openly. Only the subject of religion competes, they feel, as a primal fact of human motivation. Sex and religion, to the artists, are equally life-like and God-like. The figures that appear in the photo-pieces are selected precisely because they express the special vitality of those primal life forces—sexuality and religiosity—at their most formative and explosive stages, namely, in the prime of youth. Like artists from virtually the beginning of time, Gilbert and George employ models and direct them in studio shooting sessions toward particular poses and expressions. The artists think of their subjects as material—a kind of clay to be molded into a new image. The "campaigning artists" view these youths that appear so often in their work as both knights and procreators (fig. 10), and they cast them as the heroes of their visual sermons, carefully composed narratives conceived as moral instruction.

There is a significant if often elusive distinction to be drawn on the issue of autobiography. It may be largely because their own images appear so regularly in the works' narratives that this issue of autobiographical content remains persistent and ambiguous. The work is not about Gilbert and George, but it is about life, and theirs is the only life with which they are on intimate terms. The subjects are thus torn from the minds, hearts, and daily observations of the artists, but the meaning and impact of these subjects are of substantially more generalized implication. Certain states of mind and heart are shared as universals of the human experience and cannot be confined to one individual's behavioral circumstances. These are the universals addressed by Gilbert and George, and they strike resonant chords in many viewers despite the fact that those viewers may never have spent an evening in an English pub or walked the rose gardens of London's Temple Court. All of their subjects—whether London's office buildings or flowering branches or self-portraits or toy soldiers or working class youths—are an integral part of Gilbert and George's visual, intellectual, and spiritual world, but they should be interpreted as emblematic representations rather than as elements in the artists' private lives. It is fundamental to distinguish between Gilbert and George's personal identity and the larger meaning of the work. This is a symbolic art, not an autobiographical art.

"to do this funny thing"

At St. Martin's in early 1969 Gilbert and George presented *Our New Sculpture* (later retitled *Underneath the Arches* and finally *The Singing Sculpture*). In extremely stylized form they acted out the lyrics to the Hardy and Hudson version of Flanagan and Allan's English music hall standard, "Underneath the Arches," using only a tape recorder, a walking stick, and a glove as props. The presentation lasted about five minutes. In 1969 and 1970, and in subsequent years in various contexts, they presented *Living Sculpture with Heads* (fig. 11), in which their exposed flesh was coated with multi-colored bronze powder. The "living-pieces" have always taken different forms, sometimes as public strolling-pieces, sometimes as frozen poses (at the Stedelijk Museum, Amsterdam, in 1969 a "bronzed" pose was struck on the museum's central staircase and held for five hours), sometimes as *The Singing Sculpture*, rendering "Underneath the Arches" (at the Düsseldorf Kunsthalle in 1970 the presentation lasted eight hours on each of two consecutive days). In 1975 they created *The Red Sculpture*, with their heads, hair, necks, and hands solidly coated in bright red. This "living-piece" lasted ninety minutes and was poetically scripted, with their robot-like movements correlated to the different moods of each of nine distinct sections (e.g., "Cherry Blossom," "Bad Thoughts and Broken Hearts," "Wooden Air," "Gone," "Bloody Life and Dusty Corners," "Red Boxers"). Many of these subtitles recur as series titles for photo-pieces of the same years.

The "living sculpture" work exists on a continuum with the tradition of *tableau vivant* (from the French, literally "living picture"). Such theatrical depictions, usually presented on a stage by silent and motionless costumed participants, but also a standard entertainment at house parties of the period (a kind of charade), originated in the late eighteenth or very early nineteenth century and figured prominently in literature and drama especially in the nineteenth century. Sculpture come to life has its roots in Greek mythology—Pygmalion, king of Cyprus, made an ivory female figure which was given life for him by Aphrodite—and has been a recurrent motif in art and literature ever since. In the 1982 English film by Peter Greenaway, *The Draughtsman's Contract*, "living statues" appear and reappear as a leitmotif in the plot. According to the uncut version of the film, this plot device is based on historical fact, suggesting that in seventeenth-century England when, as now, art was more highly valued than physical labor, certain landowners, rather than expending funds to commission bronze garden sculpture, employed country louts to coat themselves in lampblack and pose as living statues. These serfs would strike static poses on pedestals or in the estate's formal gardens, thus contributing to the artifice of the highly contrived landscape setting. To particularly menacing effect in the film, the primary characters go about their daily lives unaware that the sculptures are *faux*, and the "sculptures" are in turn unobserved witnesses to the misadventures (murder and sexual intrigue) recounted in the story. There are fascinating parallels between this alleged earlier English fashion and the "living sculpture" of Gilbert and George. The artists identify strongly with the working classes and could easily project themselves in the role of "country lout," both entertaining and deceiving their gentried audience; they have consciously and consistently created a state of ambiguity between personal identity and art, between the real and the contrived; and they wish to live and die as witnesses, in almost a religious sense, to the misadventures of human experience. Although Gilbert and George are not aware of any specific precedent for "living statues" in earlier English history (and, indeed, academic specialists in the history and culture of the period also discount historical precedent), the artists certainly know the *tableau vivant* tradition and are inclined to attribute what they see as a renewed contemporary interest in this genre to the high profile of their own dedication to the form since 1969. (Greenaway, who studied art in England in the late 1960's, was present at some of the very early *Singing Sculpture* presentations by Gilbert and George at that time, and it is perfectly plausible that such memorable imagery has informed his filmmaking.)[2] The inverse of "sculpture come to life" is the living figure becoming sculptural. There is also literary precedent for the latter metaphor. Certain legends from antiquity recount the transformation of human form into stone or wood, and Lot's wife was turned into a pillar of salt. This motif often relates to a plot requirement that a character seem to be dead, such as Hermione in *The Winter's Tale*, or *Sleeping Beauty*. The concept of "living sculpture" as invented by Gilbert and George is of course quite different, since there is no transmogrification from living to sculptural form, or vice versa, in their persona. Quite the contrary, they have merged living and sculptural form in order to obliterate, rather than emphasize, the distinctions between the two.

By about 1977 the artists began to grow increasingly concerned at the narrow categorization of their work as "performance art," and they also saw the rapid popularity and media acclaim attendant on the "living sculpture" presentations as a potential trap. Although they sustained without hesitation their life roles as living sculpture, the public presentation format became less dominant in the work. Such presentations had never been the exclusive medium for their art expression; throughout these same years they worked actively in many other mediums, including videotape, bookworks, drawings, paintings, and of course photo-pieces. Accordingly, from 1977 at least to the present, they have declined invitations to recreate *The Singing Sculpture*, *Living Sculpture with Heads*, *Underneath the Arches*, or *The Red Sculpture*.

"walking along a new road"

Since 1969 Gilbert and George had incorporated photographic images in their bookworks, announcements, postal sculptures, and magazine sculptures. They had also always insisted upon careful and artful documentation of the "living sculpture" works, images which in themselves became art documents of a sort that now seem early prototypes for the later photo-pieces. They had never been interested in the single, isolated image, however, feeling that its scale was too precious and invited a connoisseur's response. To achieve scale impact, they decided to group clusters of images. They did their first wall **Photo-Pieces** in **1971**, for an exhibition at Art & Project, Amsterdam (fig. 12). These first photo-pieces were composed in geometric formations, with stepped outlines and variable interstices between frames. Both vertical and horizontal format images were employed in each piece. All black-and-white, these pieces combine flowers and foliage from park settings with portraits of Gilbert and George, usually together, almost always in "stop-action" poses, as if caught in mid-walk or mid-sentence. A timing mechanism was used for most of the early photo-pieces in which Gilbert and George appear together. In the later photo-pieces when the artists appear side by side (which is quite often), it is an illusion created by joining two or more distinct, usually studio-shot images. These first photo-pieces were untitled and always included groups of images, individually framed, composed in irregular formats. Throughout the 1971 photo-pieces the artists look very young, and the series, overall, conveys a sensibility of serenity, relaxation, happiness, and relative informality.

The announcement card for the exhibition, *Modern Rubbish*, at the Sonnabend Gallery, New York, November 1973, declared the work to be "New decorative photographic wall drinking sculptures." The work throughout **1973–1974**—series called **Any Port In A Storm**, **New Decorative Works**, **Modern Rubbish**, and **A Drinking Sculpture**—seemed to focus on drinking and drunkenness and featured glasses, bottles, liquor labels, bar interiors, and the artists as drinkers. These same subjects appeared as a regular motif in postcard works of 1972 (fig. 13), pointing the way toward the subsequent photo-pieces. There is a remarkably similar sensibility between the "found" imagery of the postcard subjects and the "invented" imagery of the photo-pieces. In this regard, it is important to know that the artists consider their postcard works as "sketches" for photo-pieces, even while they stand as complete works of art on their own. Titles of the photo-pieces from this period included *Staggering*, *Slippery Glasses*, *Gin Mist*, *Black Stare*, *Muscadet*, *Raining Gin*, *Health Mess* (fig. 14), *London Fog*, *Gin and Tonic*, *The Secret Drinker*, etc. The format of the compositions reflected on the subject matter: frames were skewed on the wall at sharp angles to one another or tilted to suggest a disoriented vision. The images were often blurred and out of focus, or smudged and spattered, or cropped tightly to provide only partial content information. The work imposed on the viewer the same kind of diminished focus that the consumption of too much alcohol imposes on the drinker. The **Inca Pisco** series of **1974**, with its title homage to a brand of Peruvian brandy, continued the same themes, but with each piece composed in the stylized form of an Aztec figure (fig. 15). Also in **1974** the artists completed the **Human Bondage** series (fig. 16), still all in black-and-white, in which Gilbert and George are depicted in physically extreme circumstances of apparent drunkenness—fallen down, reaching out, human detritus among the debris of broken glasses and liquor bottles. Each of the works is superimposed with a cross or swastika-shaped line in the form of chains or ropes or bonds. The overall format of all of the *Human Bondage* works is also in swastika shape. Alcoholism is only the literal subject of the 1973–1974 works; it stands symbolically for all forms of "bondage" to which humans are subject and, as such, bares the scars of all forms of fascistic control over individual behavior, whether political or personal. In the *Human Bondage* series Gilbert and George introduced a numbering system to identify individual pieces (and, concomitantly, to link firmly each piece in a given series one with the other, to underscore the fact that they were creating thematic series). Unlike the 1971 works, generically and individually identified simply as *Photo-Pieces*, or the 1973–1974 works which carried individual names, *Human Bondage* works (and

Fig. 12. PHOTO-PIECE. 1971. 31½ × 37⅜ in. (80 × 95 cm.).

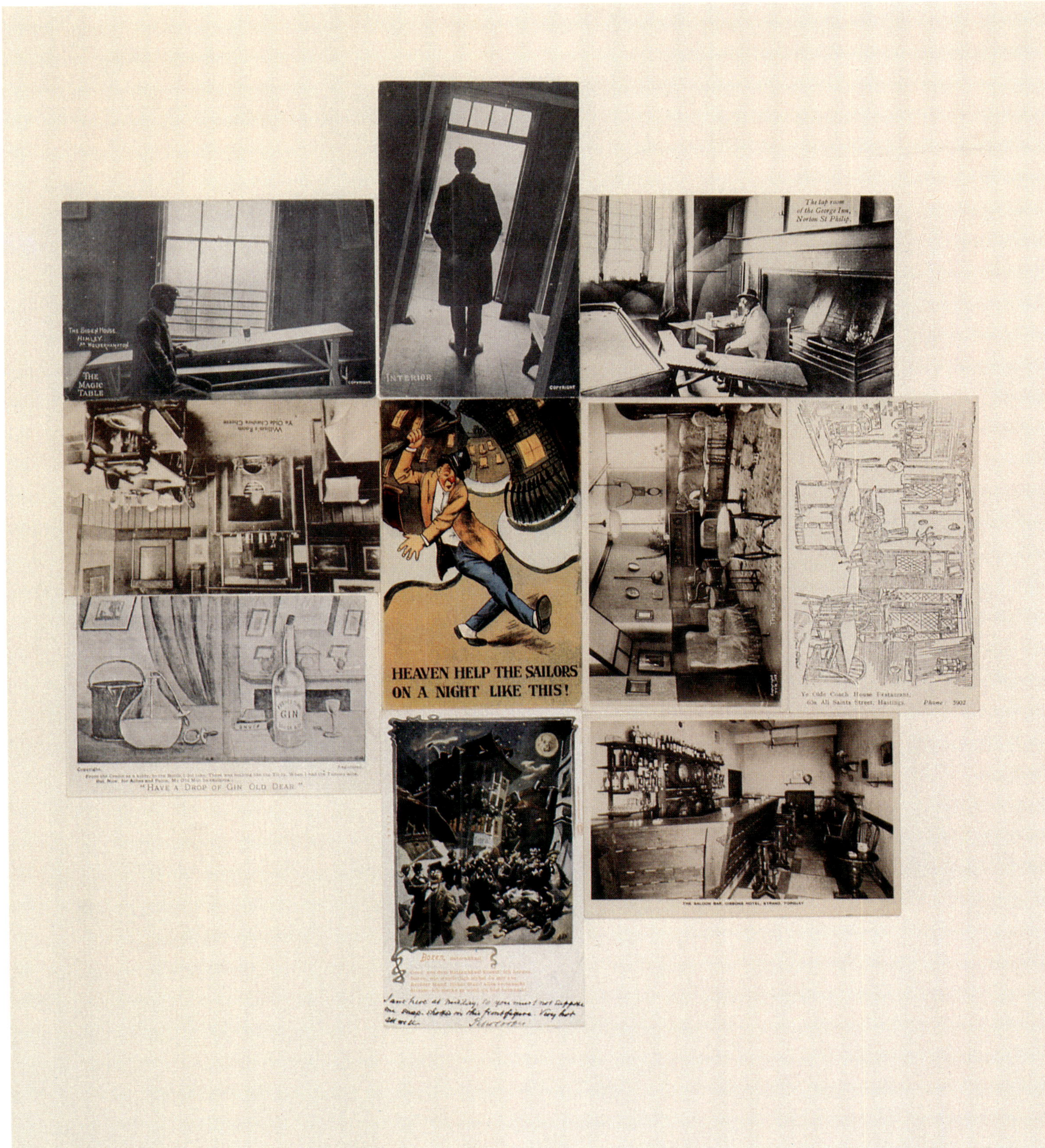

Fig. 13. POST CARD SCULPTURE. 1972. Collection of David Brown, London.

Fig. 14. HEALTH MESS. 1973.

Fig. 15. INCA PISCO B. 1974. 120⅛ × 161½ in. (305 × 410 cm.). Collection of Mr. and Mrs. Anton Herbert, Ghent, Belgium.

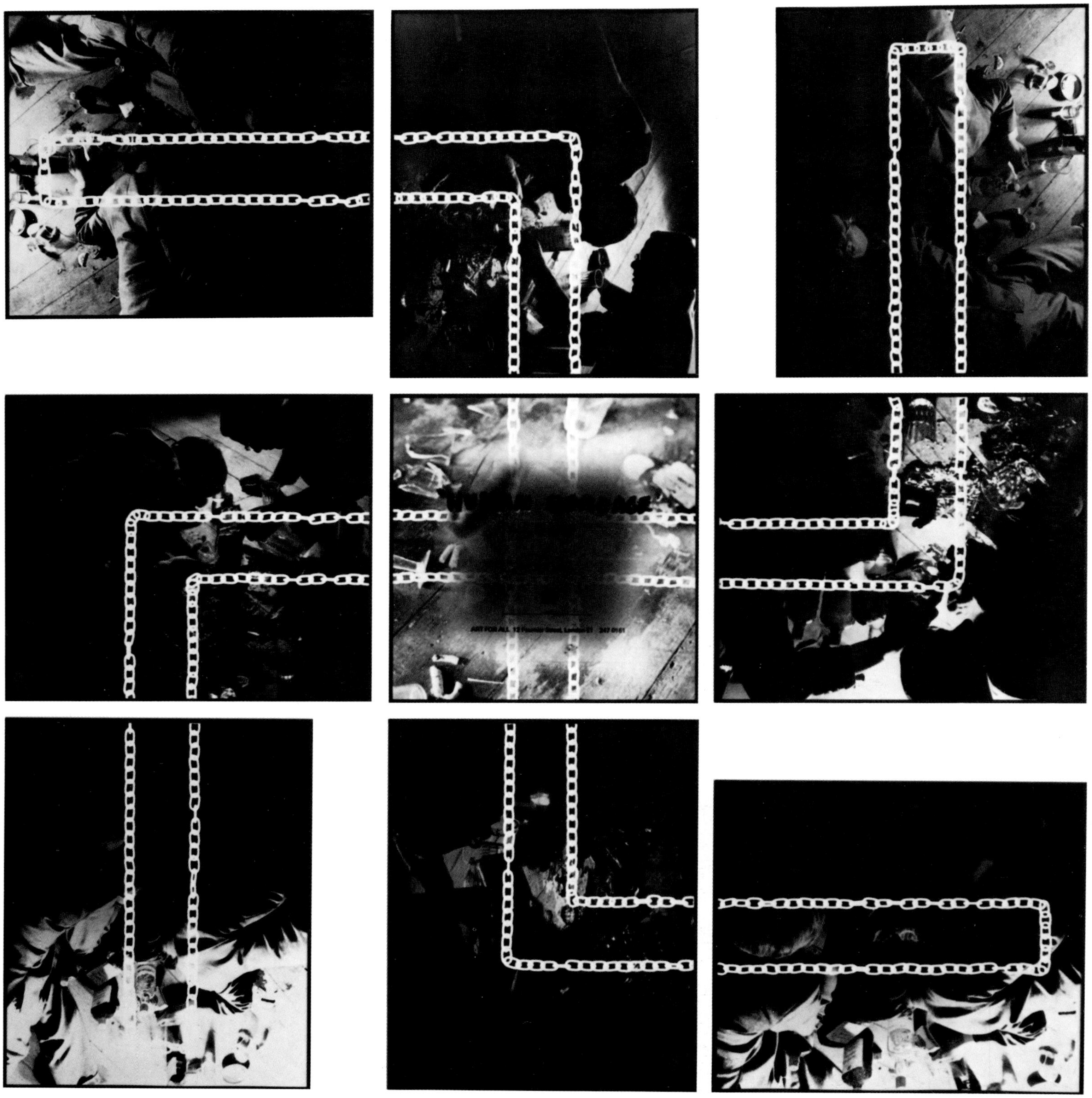

Fig. 16. HUMAN BONDAGE 5. 1974. 68½ × 68½ in. (174 × 174 cm.). Collection of the artists.

all of those in series until the 1977 *Red Morning*) were identified by a sub-number, e.g., *Human Bondage 6*.

In 1974 the color red "began to creep into" the work. Red can be seen as the predominant color in many of the postcard sculptures of 1974 (figs. 17–18), and red ink was often used in the early works for the artists' signatures. But in the later 1974 works red began to appear with regularity and to intense and specific effect. The artists wanted to add color to the work to express certain emotional feelings and, then and now, they consider red to be the most powerfully symbolic color, what they call the "color of desperation." (Not until 1980 did they expand their color palette still further.) Both the **Dark Shadow** and **Cherry Blossom** series of late **1974** show the artists' use of "desperate red." In the *Dark Shadow* works, images of the artists appear only as heads, or with some torso, and their figures are always angled in the frame. There are fragmented images of paneled walls, often striated with sun and shade, interspersed with units depicting pools and webs of simulated dripping blood (fig. 19). It is an especially stark series, filled with apprehension and confusion. *Dark Shadow 6* (fig. 20) includes superimposed portraits of Gilbert and George, so that it becomes unclear whether or not there are two individuals depicted (Gilbert appears to be wearing George's eyeglasses; George's ear conjoins with Gilbert's eye). In most of the *Cherry Blossom* works, the artists are shown sprawled on the studio floor, bodies strewn with bamboo sticks. Gilbert would pose, and George would "chuck the bamboo sticks" over him and shoot the image; and then vice versa. At this time in their lives they became involved with Oriental thought and culture; in particular, they became addicted to Chinese musicals and the martial arts. In Oriental culture the cherry blossom is the symbol of bravery, especially as it relates to the young soldier. The cherry blossom is the first flora to brave the risky spring weather, and it is the first to die. The cherry blossom has a very special symbolic place in the work of Gilbert and George. In the spring of 1971 the artists had issued a bulletin through Art & Project, Amsterdam, called *A Touch of Blossom* (fig. 21). The artists are posed, George slightly behind Gilbert, next to a blossoming cherry tree in a park, with the tree's branched petals touching each of them. They are thus brought into intimate contact only through the medium of the blossom. They are committed to the image of the flower as symbol—representing the cycle of life and death in a rapid and uniquely poignant way, and also representing open sexuality without any of the socially threatening connotations of human sexuality. The works in *Cherry Blossom* are all very tightly composed, with explosions of violence confined in box-like frames (fig. 22). The works are inscribed "Cherry Blossom" in pseudo-Oriental bamboo block print, underscoring the theatrical nature of the imagery.

Bloody Life of **1975** strips away the theatrical, posed formality of the *Cherry Blossom* series, and boldly reveals the state of utter depression which began to consume the artists in what they saw as a period of "fighting life." Most prominent in the series are the images of the artists themselves, in contorted "hiding" poses (*Bloody Life 10*) or lashing out in poses simulating Chinese martial arts movements (*Bloody Life 2* and *Bloody Life 11* [fig. 23]). It is an aggressive, desolate series, with the title being both a curse against life (in relation to the English slang meaning of "bloody") and an appeal for salvation from decadent violence (the artists report that they were thinking of the "blood of Christ" when they adopted the blood imagery). Portraits of the artists appear in very high contrast, so that their bodies seem to dissolve in light and dark. *Bloody Life* reveals an almost tangible battle to survive as physical elements against a tide of destructive forces, both internal and external. *Bloody Life 3*, in particular, illustrates the battle, with its scenes from a boxing match and images of liquor streaming into glasses, all represented in stark and crystalline light and dark. From the same year, **Bad Thoughts** encapsulates the artists' conviction that art should deal with the entire spectrum of human motivation, whether admirable or not. Gilbert and George define "bad thoughts" as destructive emotions or "thoughts one tends to be ashamed of," such as guilt, fear, anger. Although the artists do make value judgments, that is, they recognize the differences that exist between "good thoughts" and "bad thoughts," they nonetheless accept the fascinating range of such behavior as appropriate, even mandatory, for the content of their artwork. In *Bad Thoughts* one can see the artists turning inward—away from the violent exterior world of *Bloody Life*, and toward the interior, self-analytical world of the mind. They call *Bad Thoughts* "a prison of ourselves," with its repetition of boxed images of interior views (the only sign of the outside world is an occasional bare tree branch glimpsed through a windowpane) and self-portraits in profile or three-quarter views. The most prominent subject in *Bad Thoughts* is the interior of the Fournier Street house, with tightly

Fig. 17. POST CARD SCULPTURE. 1974.
Collection of Ileana and Michael Sonnabend, New York.

Fig. 18. POST CARD SCULPTURE. 1974. Art & Project, Amsterdam.

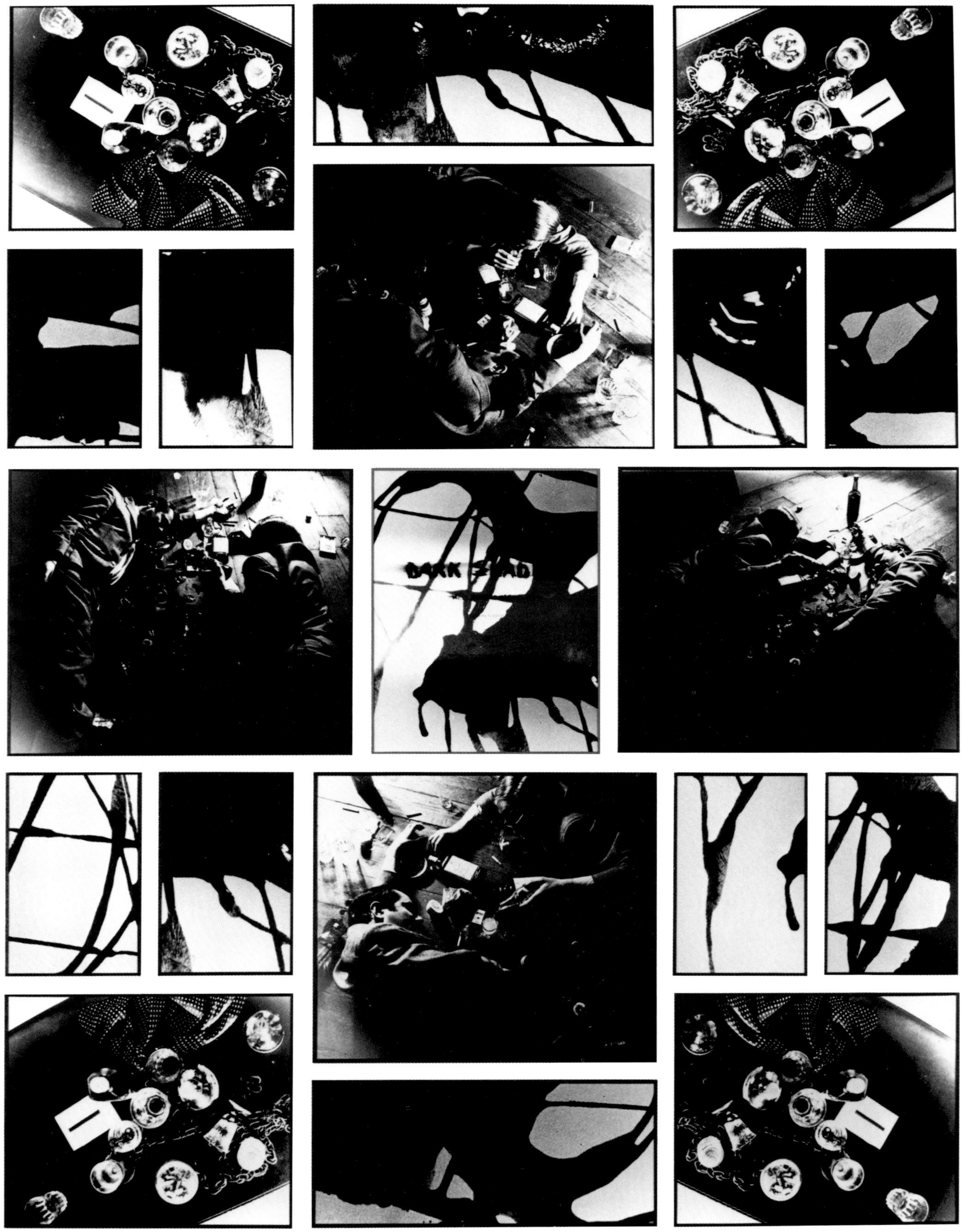

Fig. 19. DARK SHADOW 9. 1974. 83½ × 65⅜ in. (212 × 166 cm.).
Art Gallery of South Australia, Adelaide.

Fig. 20. DARK SHADOW 6. 1974. 51½ × 81½ in. (131 × 207 cm.). Collection of the artists.

Overleaf: Fig. 21. A TOUCH OF BLOSSOM, Spring 1971 (*Bulletin 47*, Art & Project, Amsterdam).

A TOUCH OF BLOSSOM. Spring 1971

With Best Wishes to You George Gilbert

the sculptors

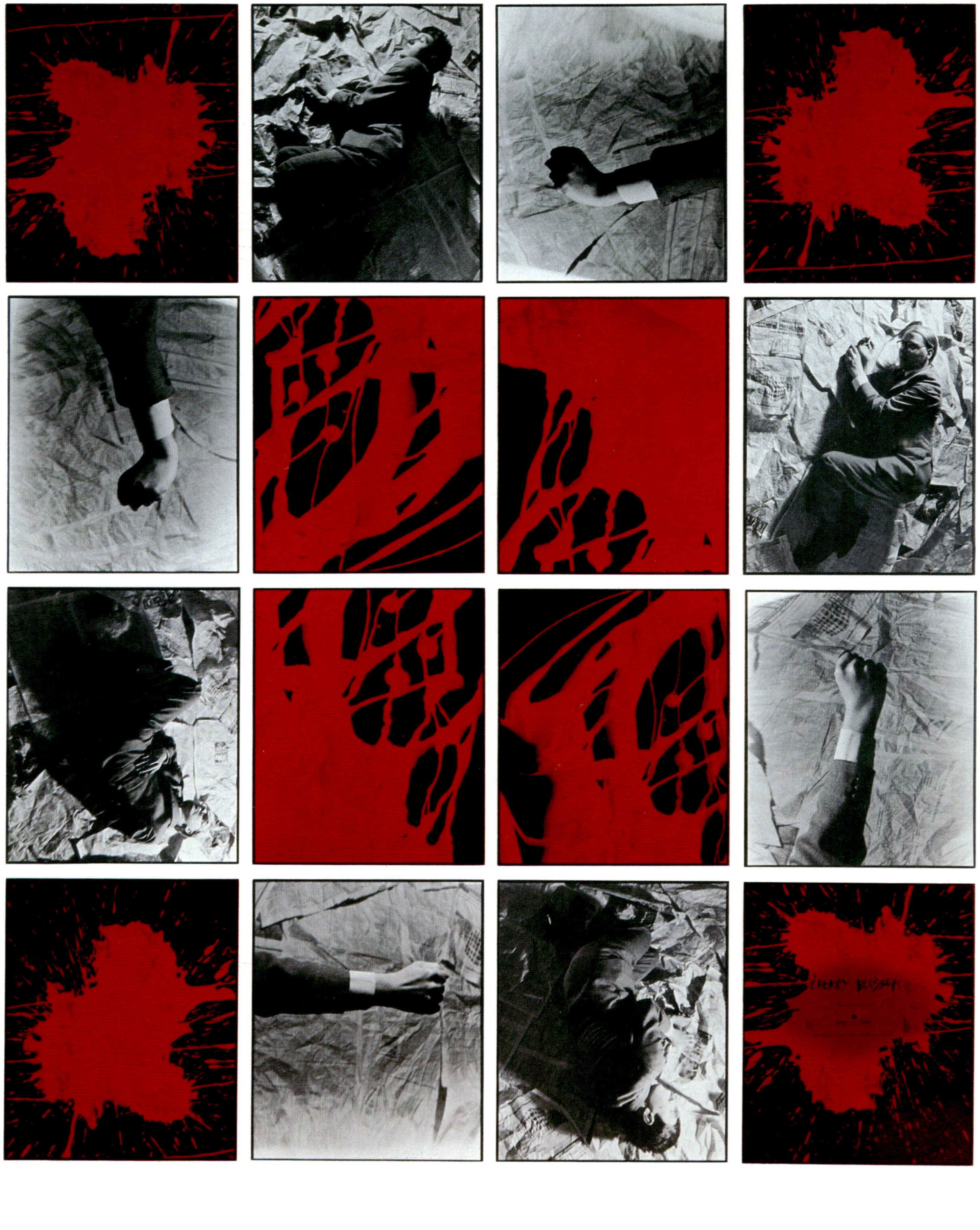

Fig. 22. CHERRY BLOSSOM 5. 1974. 96⅞ × 81⅛ in. (246 × 206 cm.).

Fig. 23. BLOODY LIFE 11. 1975. 96⅞ × 81⅛ in. (246 × 206 cm.).

cropped abstractions of its wood paneling. Like all of the series since *Dark Shadow*, *Bad Thoughts* incorporates both black-and-white and red panels.

For **Dusty Corners** of **1975** and **Dead Boards** of **1976**, the artists reverted to composing exclusively in black-and-white. The pieces are, for the first time, composed with the color gray (in symbolic reference to the "dusty" of the title of the 1975 series, as well as to the "dead" of the 1976 title), and the images are necessarily in much reduced contrast. All of the shots were taken in the Fournier Street house and, except for ambient light from the windows, there is no evidence of the outside in these images. The artists are alone in their house, a closed world, and only occasionally look out the windows in highly tentative, wistful poses. Gilbert and George consider the texts of *The Red Boxers* (figs. 24–25), an eight-part postal sculpture from 1975, to be a narrative description of the content of *Dusty Corners*:

> In the room we looked across
> The WOODEN AIR between.
>
> Leaning on the window sill awhile
> Two STONE-ISH faces on the floor.
>
> STILLNESS breathing through our
> air makes us still breathe.
>
> Back on back and shooting through
> the closed STUDY.
>
> They moved and paused a little
> Not seeing ANYTHING.
>
> And tilted, MOVED on with dry
> boards and then to STAND.
>
> Walking across the window glass
> Dry figures COME to them.
>
> Two in the CHAPEL with life
> around the suits.

Dead Boards, according to Gilbert and George, is about "the life of a board," and in the static, wooden poses of the artists there is a symbolic conjoining of the human figure and the wood panel as comparable forms.

With **Mental** of **1976**, Gilbert and George thrust themselves once again into the outside world, and all of the imagery (except for the studio poses of the artists, in which they are always shown in movement, usually walking) is exterior—cityscapes (both day and night views) and flowers. "Mental" in Britain is lower class slang for "mad" (as in, "he's gone mental"), and there is an obsessive, rigid order to the *Mental* compositions which suggests a kind of madness. The format of the pieces is based on the banner-like Crusader cross. The artists' walking poses are intended to recall the marching of Christian soldiers, and the unusual distanced views of the artists' figures within each frame underscore the sense of untouchable purity with which they romantically invest the concept of the Crusader. The artists' bodies are shown in full; they shot one another as each walked back and forth a certain prescribed distance in the studio (fig. 26). Although the theme of the series is "mental," suggesting a focus on interior thought, in fact their heads in these images seem little more than sculptures perched on the pedestals of their bodies. This is largely a product of the scale of the figures' settings: Gilbert and George seem to recede into expansive space at a great distance from the viewer, and they seem very tiny in relation to the frame, almost as if conjured in an "Alice" hallucination. *Mental* communicates quite clearly for the first time the artists' role as "campaigning artists," crusaders for progress in art and life. At the same time, *Mental* conveys a detachment from life, an elimination of personal feeling, that is not characteristic of earlier work. Much of its formality derives from the powerful, flat compositions, and the stark contrasts of black, white, and red. Even the flower panels are more iconic than lyrical in *Mental*.

In the **1977** series, **Red Morning**, the artists become explicitly political. The series expresses a fear of Communism and other forms of "fascistic" governmental control. For the only time in their work, the artists depicted themselves without their suit jackets; their white-shirted apparel conveys a "gowned" or monk-like impression of apolitical purity (in contrast with the "black shirts" or "brown shirts" of the Nazis and Fascists). The works are based on very tight order both in form and imagery. The imagery relies heavily on "fascistic cityscapes," mostly high-rise modern architecture of a disturbing order and sameness. The artists are always looking either up or down and, often, into marked light or dark. The illusion of sky or landscape imagery was created by shooting reflections in puddles on the street. Street debris, "muck," or rubbish are frequent images, clearly foreshadowed in several related postcard sculptures from 1976 (figs. 27–28). *Red Morning* is notable as the first series in which the artists established the gridded, abutted-frame format which has remained standard for the photo-pieces ever since. (The black metal frame, absolutely integral to the aesthetic conception of the photo-pieces, was designed by the artists to keep the work as flat to the wall as possible.) Gilbert and George

Fig. 24. "ANYTHING" (Detail of Cover), second in the eight-part Postal Sculpture, *The Red Boxers*, 1975.

Fig. 25. "STILLNESS" (Detail of Cover), fifth in the eight-part Postal Sculpture, *The Red Boxers*, 1975.

Fig. 26. MENTAL 1. 1976. 145⅝ × 122 in. (370 × 310 cm.).

Fig. 27. A POST-CARD SCULPTURE. 1976.
Collection of Fried, Frank, Harris, Shriver, and Jacobson, New York.

Fig. 28. A POST-CARD SCULPTURE. 1976. Art & Project, Amsterdam.

wanted to consolidate the images to emphasize the mural-like quality of the works, to obliterate perception of individual units as somehow isolated one from the other. This segmented, grid format of the photo-pieces derived equally from philosophical and pragmatic motives. The artists view the world as having universal, natural divisions: they see life as evolving serially, step by step, year by year, almost as a house is built brick by brick (one of the 1971 drawings from *The General Jungle* series was entitled *The Total Mystery of Each Man-Layed-Brick* [fig. 29]). They see everything, both natural and constructed, as being composed of sections based on discipline and order. They wanted to produce their pieces at large scale and in conjoined units to reflect their "driven sense of sectioning." At the same time, precisely because of the large scale of the work, they consciously sought a practical means of assembling and disassembling mural-sized pieces. In this regard the format evolved very much out of the artists' early drawn works. In 1969 they had begun to make large-scale drawings, usually charcoal on paper, always self-portraits in landscape or interior settings. The drawings were ordinarily designed for specific installations, forming a continuous narrative around a room (and with *The Bar* of 1972 [fig. 30], also covering the ceiling). The 1974 *The Tuileries* (fig. 31) included furniture as well, constructed of wood and then covered with paper and drawn upon, to form a total environment. Because the drawings were mural-sized and somewhat fragile, the artists decided to make the works in a grid format so that the sheets could be folded in upon themselves for ease of handling and storage. The resulting grid demarcation is a clear and integral aspect of the works' impact (fig. 32). The style of these drawings is very free and expressionistic, with a dense webbing of lines creating an overall field of light and dark, very much like wallpaper (an effect intended by the artists). The image of the artists is often camouflaged by the linear network, as if Gilbert and George were lost in the landscape. Although these drawings comprised their primary means of visual expression only between 1970 and 1975, drawing, more generally, has been of consistent importance to the artists and is almost always the initial form in which they work out their ideas.

Red Morning also set the style of the artists' titling for all future works. While units in preceding series were individually identified by sequential numbers, with *Red Morning* Gilbert and George began to sub-identify individual works with single-word titles: *Red Morning Dirt*, *Red Morning Blood*, *Red Morning Scandal*, *Red Morning Hell*, *Red Morning Hate*, *Red Morning Violence*, *Red Morning Drowned*. In some of the early drawings and, especially, in the 1973–1974 photo-piece series, the artists used one- or two-word titles. Gilbert and George feel strongly that a work can be better with a proper title, and they consider a work's title a crucial part of the whole of the piece. But they finally and definitively arrived at one-word titles for the photo-pieces when they realized that titles, most importantly, could provide a clue to the work's meaning, and were also a way of firmly fixing the image for the viewer. As writers and poets, which Gilbert and George have undeniably been from the beginning, their titling assumes an eloquence which forms an integral aspect of the work's impact. Since the titles always appear on the face of the work, usually in the lower right panel, they are reinforced as an essential feature of the visual impression as well as of the content.

One of the most powerful series created by Gilbert and George, the **Dirty Words** pieces of **1977** bring the photo-pieces to full maturity. The content of the series is extraordinary for its culminating authority and intensity of vision. The works are aggressively sociopolitical and, for the first time, seem to suggest that the artists are taking an almost activist position in confronting the world. *Dirty Words* consistently incorporates as subjects figures other than the artists (relatively rare in earlier series), and focuses on the disturbing ambiguity between the real and the artificial. Real street scenes are juxtaposed with studio shots of toy soldiers or carefully arranged compositions of newspaper debris. The hallmark of each piece in the series is the graffito image usually appearing in the top four panels. The artists called the series *Dirty Words* not in the sexual sense of "dirty," but with the suggestion of tainted, corrupt, or destructive political or social forces dominant in the world. Contrasting with the anarchic content of the series is the formal clarity of the series' compositions; all are arranged in a post and lintel construction (to suggest a door or gateway), and the material is strictly ordered. With this work the artists feel they were irrevocably "kicked out of the house" and into the world, a process begun in *Mental* and continued through *Red Morning*. *Dirty Words* is their consummate expression of modern life in all its palpable desperation, with tramps, the military, crowds, Blacks, Indians, cityscapes, rain all symbolizing their observation that "everybody is so desperate." The titles of the works

Fig. 29. THE TOTAL MYSTERY OF EACH MAN-LAYED-BRICK, from *The General Jungle*. 1971. Charcoal on paper. 110¼ × 88⅝ in. (280 × 225 cm.). Sonnabend Gallery, New York.

Fig 30. THE BAR 1. 1972. Charcoal on paper. Installation View, Anthony d'Offay Gallery, London.
(Drawings now in the permanent collection of the Musée national d'art moderne, Centre Georges Pompidou, Paris.)

Fig. 31. THE TUILERIES. 1974. Charcoal on paper. Installation View, Art & Project, Amsterdam. (Drawings now in the permanent collection of the Museum Boymans-Van Beuningen, Rotterdam.)

Fig. 32. THERE WERE TWO YOUNG MEN WHO DID LAUGH, from *There Were Two Young Men*. 1971. Charcoal on paper. Approx. 94½ in. (240 cm.) high. Collection of Gian Enzo Sperone, Rome.

in the series all parallel the graffito inscription of each: *Bent, Cunt, Bollocks, Prostitute Poof, Piss, Lick, Fucked Up, Are You Angry or Are You Boring?, Fuck, Cunt Scum, Bent Shit Cunt, Wanker, Smash the Reds, Prick Ass, Bummed, Queer, Communism, Angry.*

Subsequent to the *Dirty Words*, Gilbert and George no longer worked in categorized series. Although they continued to produce bodies of work with a clear unity of thematic content and compositional style, ordinarily in response to specific exhibition plans, they did not group the works under formal series titles. They continued their program of unique titling for each work, however. The titles of the **1978** works almost always include the article "the" and a descriptive noun: *The Queue, The Branch, The Alcoholic, The Sitters, The Office* (fig. 33), *The Tree, The Building, The Decorators, The Penis, The Moon* (there are a few exceptions in the group, such as *Taxi, Day, Paki*, and *Morning*). The titling underscores the intentional universal symbology of the subjects: "The Office" becomes a generic for all such office buildings everywhere, and does not apply uniquely to the specific building depicted. A few of these works are all black-and-white, but most are done in black-and-white and red. The color composition tends to vary from that of earlier works. Red segments are mostly confined to rows (rather than dyed in single units or blocks of units in a more scattered, abstract or checkerboard fashion, as in the *Dirty Words*). Very often in these pieces the red color applies to those sections with images of Gilbert and George, or to those with images of tree branches, an especially common motif in the 1978 works. The banded application of color in these works produces an effect of strong geometrical clarity, underscored by the extremely hierarchical imagery consistent to the series. There is an overriding impression of quiet passivity in these works, as if the artists were disengaging from the active anger of *Dirty Words* and were becoming intensely cautious observers of the world around them.

In the **1980** works black-and-white is used more consistently for the entire composition; imagery tends to be more consolidated (closely cropped faces, details of sculptural or architectural elements, iconic portraits of themselves and of other people); the mood of the works becomes both more lyrical and more religious. There are a number of lovely "landscape" views in the 1980 works, including *Aldgate, Fournier Snow* (fig. 34), *Spitalfields*, and *Sunset*. "Black" references appear with some regularity, as in *Black Jesus, Black Buds, Black Day*, and several works feature Christ figures (fig. 35). *Death, War*, and *Fighter* all depict dramatic details of bronze war memorial statuary in London. *Waiting, Praying, Up*, and *Crusade* cast the artists in the role of Christian contemplatives, looking toward both worldly and afterlife salvation. *Depression, Misery*, and *Hellish* see Gilbert and George turned inward, delving into the psychological terrors of selfhood and interpersonal relationships. *Local Person, Mad* (titled, according to the artists, to describe not the subject but "the madness induced in the viewer when looking at the subject"), and *Mullah* (fig. 36) focus tightly on the "faces" of other figures, mapping what Gilbert and George call the "landscape of the human visage." *Gilbert and George*, the only explicit declaration of self-portraiture in the artists' work (by virtue of its title), like *Black Church Face* and *Angels*, crops the figures' images tightly to suggest the absence of head (as opposed to face); the artists always draw a distinction between head (i.e., brain, intellect, control) and face (i.e., unsocialized appearance, truth, reality, eyes), and often transform such subjects into simple masks with continuous possibilities both formally and contextually. *Patriots* (fig. 37), *Leather Workers*, and *Britisher* all look toward working class youths as heroes of contemporary life. The series of works dating from this period is astounding in quantity—it was one of the most prolific years in the artists' history—and in range and intensity. Madness and death are the prevalent motifs, always approached with reverence and apparent calm acceptance. It may be that the passage of a human lifetime is more compelling to Gilbert and George since their own aging process and the nagging reality of physical decay are made visual in a progressive way in the chronological self-portraits depicted in their work. Certainly, funerary subjects, poses, and ideas recur in the photo-pieces as central motifs (figs. 38–39).

The visual qualities of the work changed rather dramatically for the **1981–1982** pieces, largely because of innovations in both technical and compositional devices: photograms and drawn images were added to the artists' repertory; there was great emphasis on overlapping images and complex superimpositions; a much greater variety of color was used, and several colors might appear in a single work; narrative content became more explicit and more expository; sexual imagery was used more graphically; certain of the works adopted a "cartoon-like" style (derived from photograms and their black outlining that the artists call "sausages"); the works

Fig. 33. THE OFFICE. 1978. 71¼ × 59¼ in. (181.5 × 150.6 cm.).
Collection of the artists.

Fig. 34. FOURNIER SNOW. 1980. 71¼ × 98¾ in. (181.5 × 251 cm.).
Anthony d'Offay Gallery, London.

Fig. 35. TREE JESUS. 1980. 95 × 79 in. (242 × 200.8 cm.).
Sonnabend Gallery, New York.

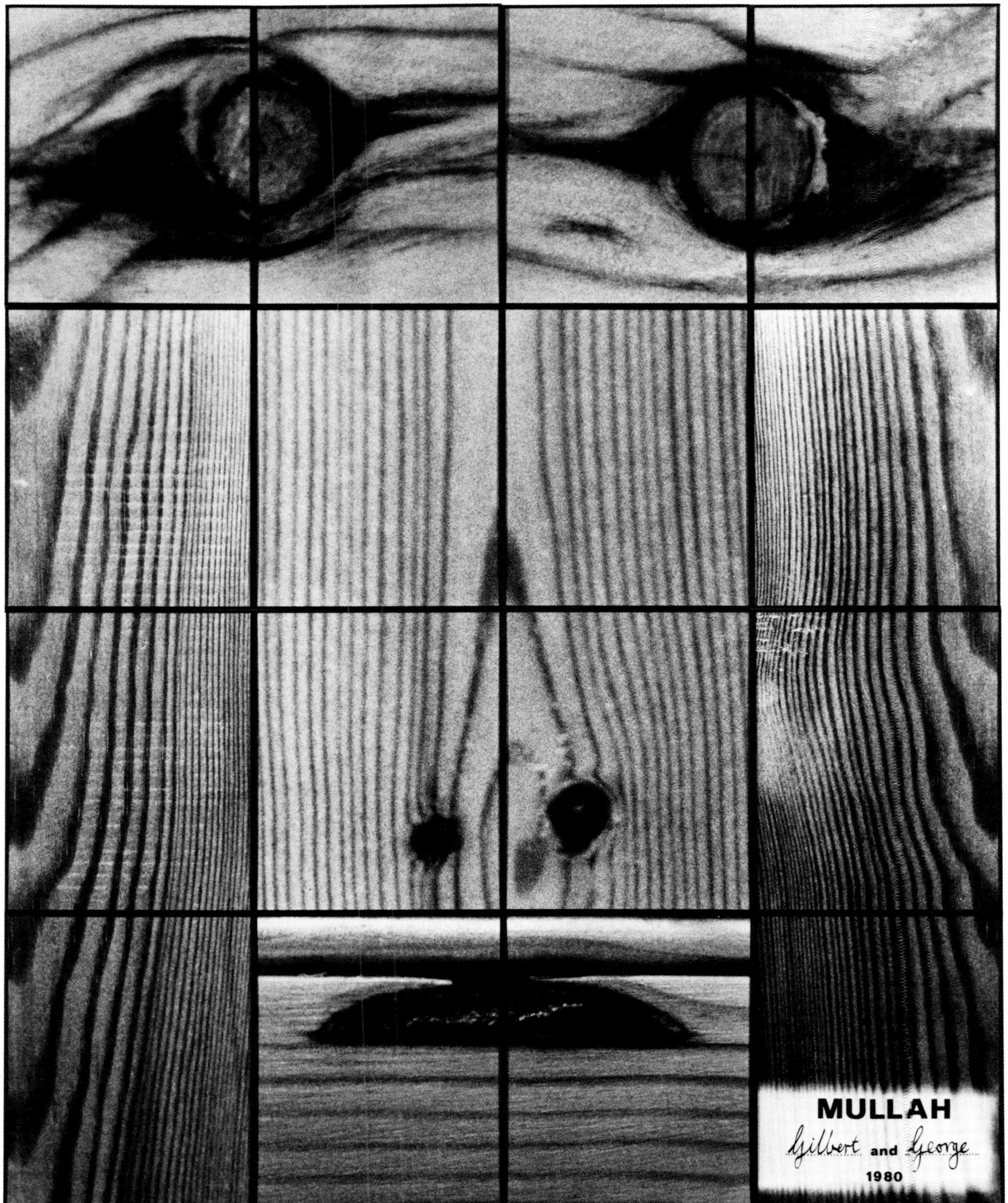

Fig. 36. MULLAH. 1980. 95 × 79 in. (242 × 200.8 cm.).
Collection of Massimo and Francesca Valsecchi, Milan and London.

Fig. 37. PATRIOTS. 1980. 71¼ × 118½ in. (181.5 × 301.2 cm.).
Collection of Martin Sklar, New York.

Fig. 38. DEAD GUARDS. 1980. 71¼ × 59¼ in. (181.5 × 150.6 cm.).
David Bellman Gallery, Toronto.

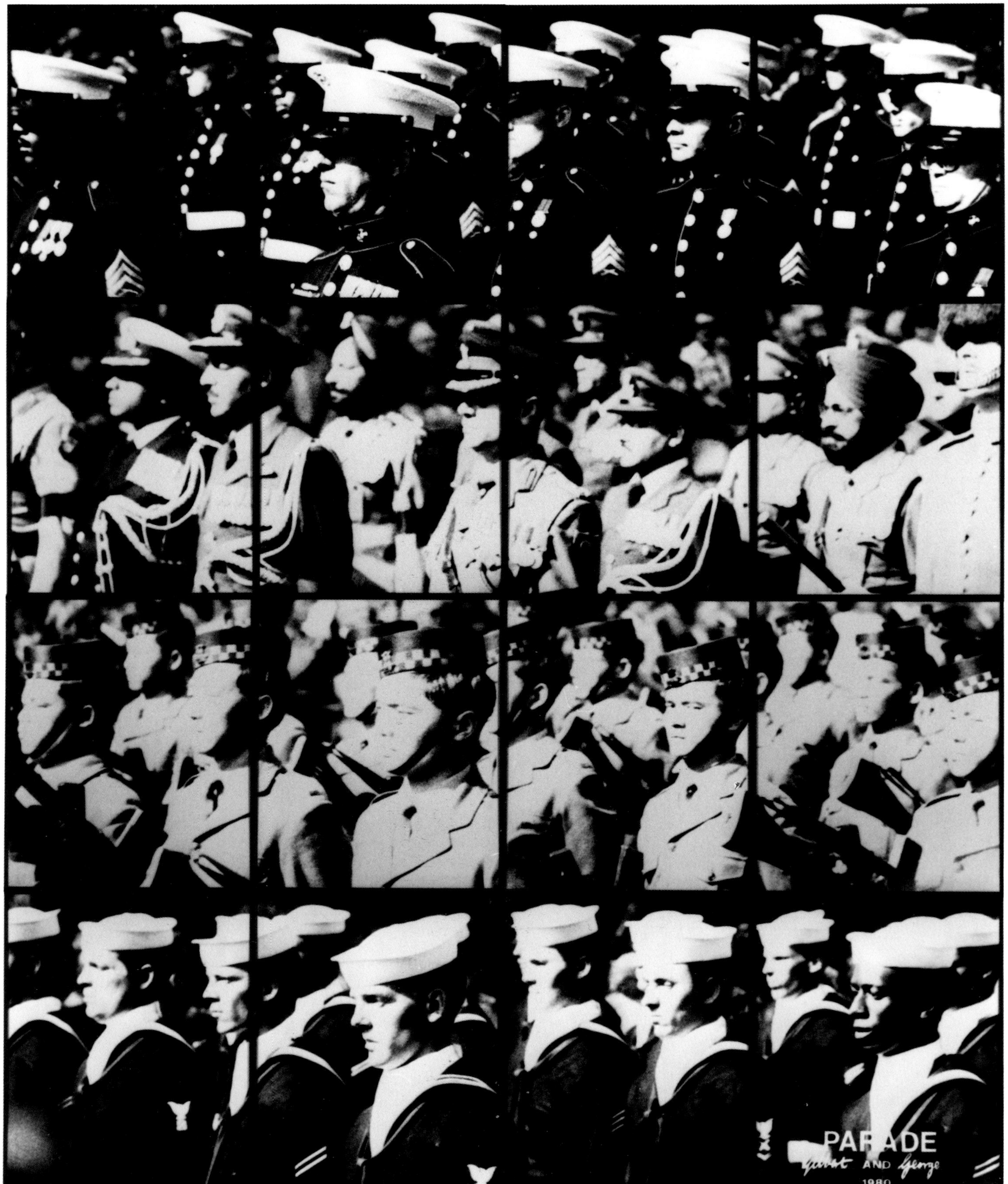

Fig. 39. PARADE. 1980. 95 × 79 in. (242 × 200.8 cm.).
Collection of Mr. and Mrs. Robert J. Dodds III, Pittsburgh.

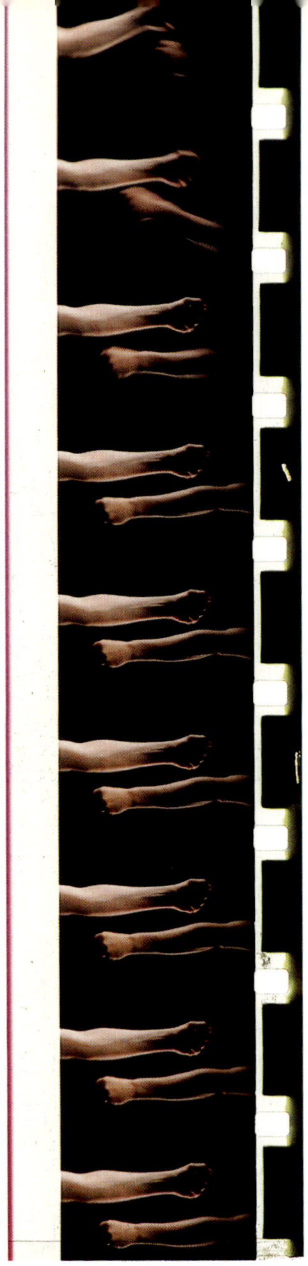

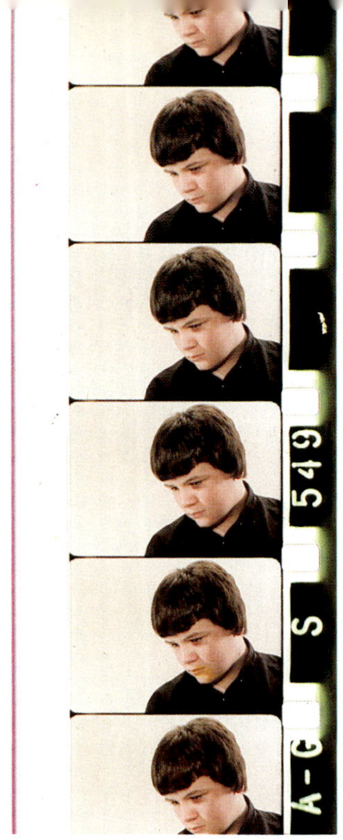

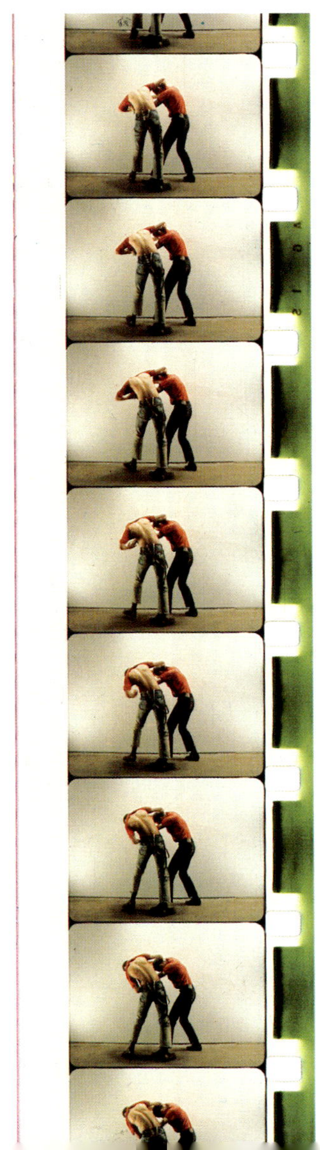

Fig. 40. THE WORLD OF GILBERT & GEORGE, 1981, Film Stills.

became even larger in size; there is much greater reliance on depictive color, often in surprisingly vivid hues. Like devotional or pedagogical art from earlier periods, many of these 1982 works rely on the concept of "simultaneous narrative," that is, the same subject appearing in varying pose or form in multiple chapters of a given narrative. Gilbert and George wanted to "pack the piece with content," "to say *more* in a single piece," "to combine subjects." In short, they wanted to deliver an extended sermon in visual form. In a work such as *Life Without End*—a monumental, culminating work of enormous formal complexity and inventiveness, a kind of coda to the artists' lives and their body of work to date—there is a continuous though scarcely linear narrative based on discrete but overlapping fragments. The narrative unravels as if in a filmic storyboard, with episodes extended in planar fashion from left to right, and with the central characters (Gilbert and George) woven through a wide range of experiences without any sacrifice to the formal integrity of the unitary work of art. Indeed, in content and visual sensibility *Life Without End* is very closely related to the artists' 1981 film, *The World of Gilbert & George* (fig. 40).

"we are sometimes a little tired"

Gilbert and George do not make art every day as a matter of course. Because they tend to work in series, they produce a body of work in a concentrated time period, almost always in response to a specific exhibition deadline. When they are physically producing the photo-pieces, they work a harrowing schedule, often beginning in the studio at dawn and working well past midnight for several weeks at a time. Even in these times they sustain their roles as "living sculpture," dressing for the day's studio activity in worn versions of their familiar uniform (shirts, ties, and jackets). Between these actual "production" periods they are always working, of course, in the sense of conceptualizing, drawing, absorbing information, and gathering imagery. They never rest from their art mission, and they consider each day a day of art exploration, what they call "a frightful foray into the soul of mankind." They constantly search their souls and scavenge the streets, seeking the "visions" that comprise the imagery of the photo-pieces. Once they enter the studio (which, tellingly, they refer to as a workshop) adjoining their house at the back garden, they become virtual automatons. They maintain a rigid working schedule which is as much physically as mentally demanding. All of the photo-pieces are initially conceived in drawn form, first with a rough color sketch, then with a much more detailed, gridded and numbered diagram, and finally with a definitive color plan (figs. 41–43). As the photo-pieces got ever more complex, these drawn diagrams became increasingly crucial to the accurate production of the finished work since the process of printing the individual parts is substantially "blind." Without the drawn diagram as a guide or maquette, the artists could not correctly abut or overlap images from one frame to the next. By the time they get to the studio, they have already completed the individual diagrams and amassed all of the necessary raw materials. Their supplies are on hand and, predictably, ordered to a point of madness. On one level, it is a physical, mechanical, step-by-step procedure which is laborious, precise, and time-consuming. They are utterly compulsive about the technical execution of the photo-pieces, and they have designed special equipment to accommodate their particular needs. Having produced tens of thousands of prints for photo-pieces since 1971, they have very much routinized the process and mechanized their tasks as workmen or technicians. At the same time, however, the process itself stimulates new ideas and innovative techniques. Like "automatic writing," form and content evolve inseparably. As each piece comes to life, the artists visualize fresh conjunctions and startling potential variations. Each work is unique; the artists never use the same image twice. The "inventory" of available imagery is staggering. For their 1983 Sonnabend Gallery exhibition, which included forty-two works, for instance, the artists took approximately 16,000 shots in the course of one year. They print all of their shots into contact sheets (fig. 44) and sort and color-code them according to subject: self-images, studio shots of other people, plants, flowers, trees, insects, and other organic materials, urban views, and architectural/sculptural details. In the past they have worked from raw materials toward the final conception of the photo-piece. In other words, they accumulated thousands of image subjects and then began to make conceptual drawings of specific compositions derived from the existing imagery. When they set out "to dredge these images out of existence," as they describe their image-seeking missions, they of course

Fig. 41. FIRST SKETCH for *Life Without End*. 1982.
Photo dyes, India ink, and watercolor on paper. $11\frac{5}{8} \times 32\frac{15}{16}$ in. (29.5×83.6 cm.).

Fig. 42. DEFINITIVE SKETCH (Gridded and Numbered) for *Life Without End*. 1982.
India ink on paper. $11\frac{5}{8} \times 32\frac{15}{16}$ in. (29.5×83.6 cm.).

Fig. 43. DEFINITIVE SKETCH (Color Plan) for *Life Without End*. 1982.
Photo dyes and India ink on paper. 12×33 in. (30.5 x 83.8 cm.).

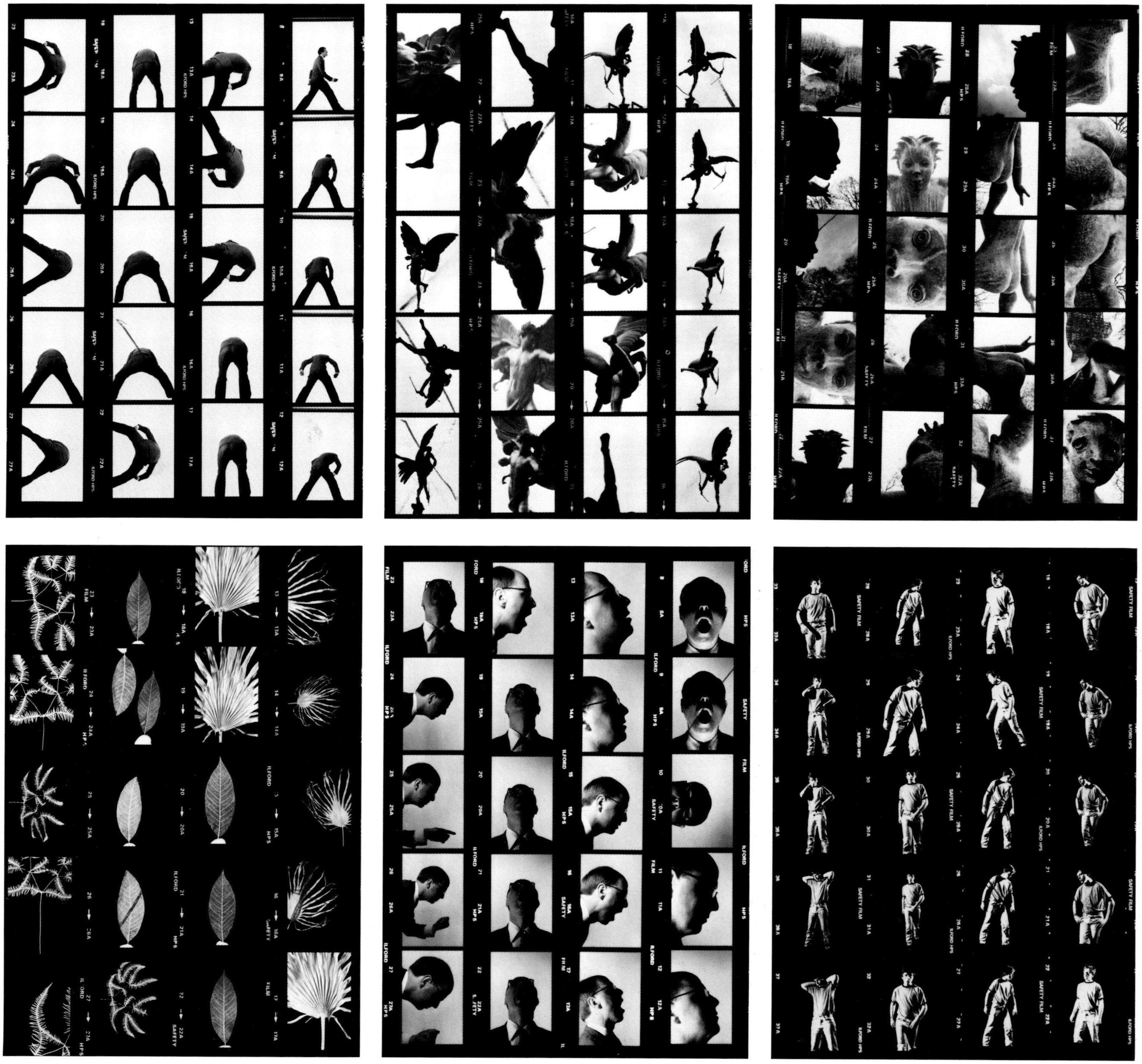

Fig. 44. CONTACT SHEETS.

have a general idea of what kinds of images they want for the pieces, that is, what a particular set or series is intended to convey as a theme or motif. But ultimate compositions have been determined very much by the given materials assembled at the time. Once the conceptual sketch has been satisfactorily refined, the scale diagram is produced, with true color applied. Only when the complete set of diagrams is finished do the artists go into the studio to begin the production of the actual photo-pieces. All of the work involved is done by hand, including the application of color with cloths. In the earlier photo-pieces images never overlapped from frame to frame, and color was dyed to the individual print, that is, held discretely within a single frame. One or more units of a given piece might be dyed red, for instance, but the color would apply to the total print, not to the isolated subject. Since 1980, however, images have overlapped frames and color has become depictive (though not necessarily descriptive) rather than panel-discrete, thus spreading across frames.

Gilbert and George report that in future they intend to organize their compositions more precisely in advance. Since the 1982 work, the photo-pieces have become monumental in scale and much more elaborate and complex in imagery. To avoid becoming overwhelmed by having almost too much image material at hand, the artists intend to alter their working method by conceptualizing the photo-pieces more fully and concretely before accumulating specific subject matter. In other words, they plan to produce rough sketches of proposed compositions first, and only then set out to find the specific shots that will fit their planned compositional needs. Instead of working from the raw imagery to the composition, they will work from the composition to the specific images in order to emphasize compositional values, narrative clarity, and emotional intensity.

In the earlier photo-pieces Gilbert and George tried to be invisible artists. Not unlike tourists, they discovered and shot images in the streets, at public events and entertainments, or in parks and at national landmarks and monuments. They worked both day and night, almost always in London and its immediate environs. When they wanted a pastoral scene they went to London's public gardens (rather than going into the country), where they found blossoms and trees, branches and greenery. They shot people and crowd or street scenes without the subjects' knowledge, often by using a telephoto lens. Not infrequently, such shots were taken from upper-story windows in public buildings or from the second-story window of their house on Fournier Street, as is evident from the angle at which figures are depicted. Always, they shot one another, either in the house's wood-paneled interiors (see the series *Bad Thoughts* and *Dusty Corners*, both 1975, and *Dead Boards*, 1976, in which, indeed, the house itself became a kind of subject) or in the studio (*Mental*, 1976, and *Red Morning*, 1977). Although this pattern of studio modeling for views of one another had been established from a very early date, it was not until 1980 that they first posed other figures in studio shots. *Stream* (fig. 45), 1980, was the first photo-piece to feature a posed and studio-shot figure other than themselves. It is unique, too, in that the subject was a friend and fellow artist, Andrew, who is also the subject of *Shame* from the same year, since in most instances their studio subjects are not known to them. Having shot Andrew in the studio, it became clear to the artists that they could obtain greater aesthetic control over their subjects by directing poses in the studio context or, alternatively, going into the streets to shoot subjects with their permission, thus gaining the capacity for close-ups, directed poses, and specific angles that were impossible from the vantage of the anonymous, invisible artist. The subjects in the 1980 *Mad*, *Local Person*, and *Fallen Leaves* were all street people who agreed to pose in situ for the artists.

In 1980, too, Gilbert and George dramatically expanded their palette. Investigating the effects of color as spiritual equivalents, they first used yellow, which appears alone or in combination with red-dyed panels in several 1980 pieces (the first all-yellow piece was *Waiting*). In 1980–1982 they began to use an even wider range of colors—green, blue, violet, orange, pink—and gold leaf as well (actually a copper-based metallic appliqué). The expansion of their palette seems somehow to have liberated them from color-discrete segments as well, and the works exploded with a rainbow of expressively symbolic color. In their film, *The World of Gilbert & George*, the narration accompanying images of rotating yellow and white chrysanthemums (fig. 46) intones ". . . with white cleanliness magnificent and yellow wellborn educated calm . . .," thus ascribing rather specific metaphorical implications to particular color choices. Seeking still greater range, they also went back to the use of photograms in 1980. As early as 1972 they had experimented with photograms (fig. 47), doing a number of photo-pieces based on photogrammed images of drinking glasses, ferns, and

Fig. 45. STREAM. 1980. 95 × 79 in. (242 × 200.8 cm.).
Collection of Lucio Amelio, Naples, Italy.

Fig. 46. POWER AND GLORY. 1980. 71¼ × 118½ in. (181.5 × 301.2 cm.). Collection of Dr. and Mrs. Phillip T. George, Miami, Florida.

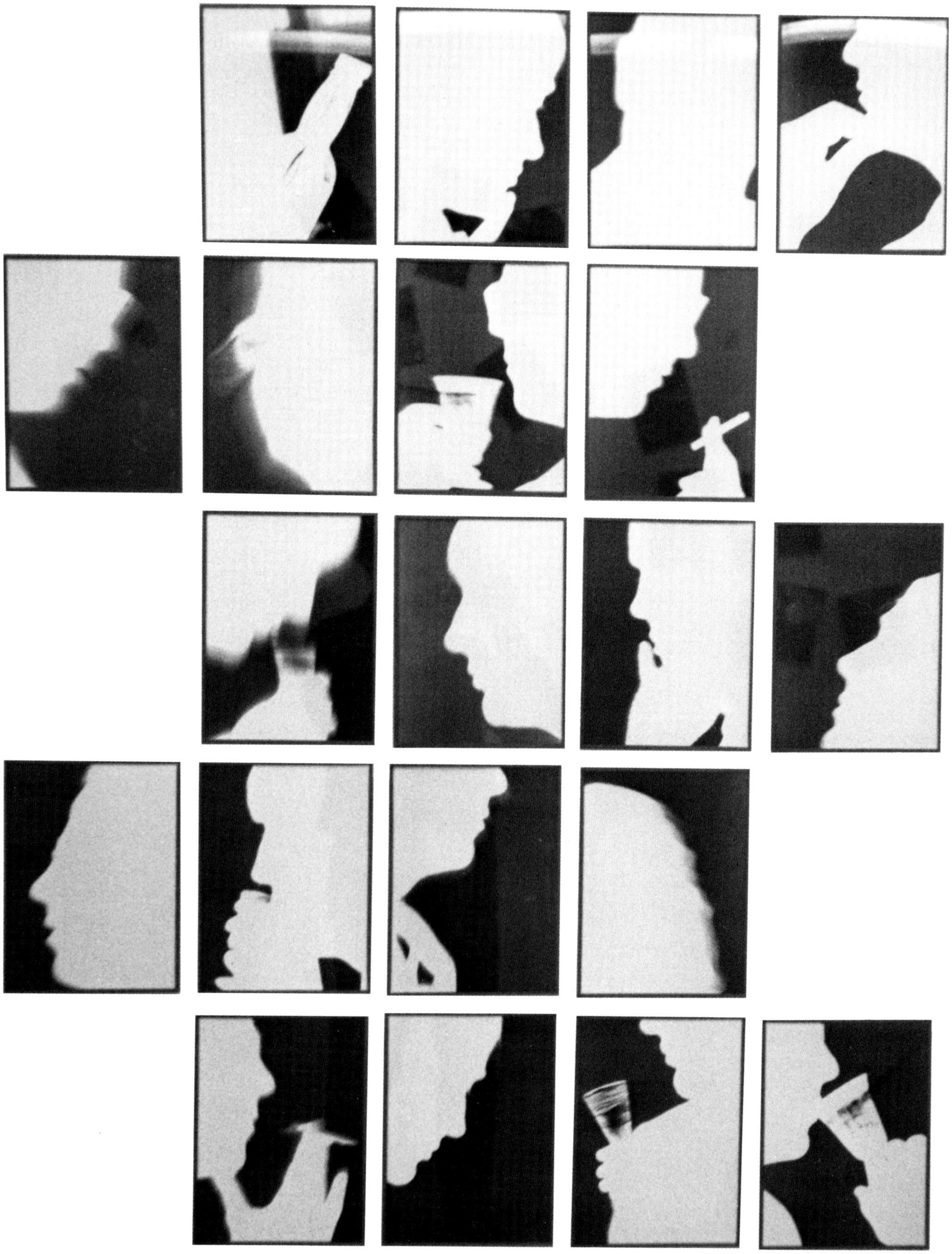

Fig. 47. IN THE SHADOW OF THE GLASS. 1972. Approx. 50 × 39½ in. (127 × 100.5 cm.).

''silhouetted'' profiles of their own heads. *Lions* was the first in these later series to employ photograms, which the artists now create by cutting out cardboard templates—a ''pattern'' placed between the source of light and the photosensitive paper, preventing exposure of specified portions of the surface. It is the cut-away portion, the ''negative image,'' which light penetrates and thus develops on the paper. They were looking for a way ''to smack out a piece in the flash of an eye,'' not to think about it very much but to fix an image instantaneously. Subsequently, they found photograms effective not just for single imagery but in combination with photographed imagery, to provide detail where it does not already exist or to add abstract form to an otherwise realistic subject (for instance, in *Forgiveness*, the raindrops—later superimposed with gold leaf—and the script ''forgiveness'' are photograms, while the two figures and the Eros monument from Piccadilly Circus are photographs). They almost always do hand-cut templates for photograms but occasionally now, as in the 1972 works, they photogram directly from found materials (in *Speaking Youth* the figure's head and torso are a mask but his underarm hair was made by photogramming whisks off the household broom).

''there is a little more to the story''

Gilbert and George are not photographers and their work is not photography. They use images of their own making exclusively. With the exception of the postcard sculptures, there are no appropriated images in their art. The images they use—whether black-and-white, hand-colored, or gilded—can be categorized as photographs only in the most literal of definitions. It is true that they call these works photo-pieces, but the photographs, as such, are only the tools and raw materials with which the art work is forged, just as a painter's brush, oil, and canvas are not the art work but only its materials and technical medium. Gilbert and George think and see and live in three dimensions. They accept as integral parts of the material art work their cumulative years of individual being; their walks and double-decker bus rides around London; their keen observation of the fragmented details that comprise people, things, and ideas (''the nature of our looking''); their studio modeling sessions; their conversational dialogue with friends; their love and goodness, and their anger and tempers; the achingly expressive drawings they make as sketches for the photo-pieces; the compulsive organization and coding of contact sheets; the grueling weeks of physical and emotional labor in making the art; the exhausting days of designing an installation and hanging the works; the exhilarating and sometimes maddening experience of submitting the work to public scrutiny; the frustration at being misunderstood through what many observers perceive to be an odd, almost perversely arrogant indulgence in obfuscation and opaqueness, despite their conviction that they and their work are presented with absolute clarity and directness; the delight at an unknown viewer's revelatory connection with a particular work; and, perhaps most of all, the explosive schizophrenia of being Gilbert and George, two determined to be one, alternating between manic and depressive, aspiring toward the most sincere religiosity in their life and work, clinging desperately to a faith in progress and morality, and yet descending into hell and despair and often bizarre confrontation with the real world more often than they would like. Above all, their obsession is to become Art:

> Is to become an artist to be reborn, or is it a condition of life? Coming slowly over a person like the daybreak. It brings the art-ability to do this funny thing and shows you new possibilities for feeling and scratching at oneself and surroundings, setting standards, making you go into every scene and every contact, every touching nerve and all your senses. . . .

Taken in this context, it is understandable that Gilbert and George prefer to define their work as sculpture—something tactile, fully dimensional, constructed out of time and mind and materials in an identifiable and yet infinitely mysterious process. One definition of sculpture, in its verb usage, is ''to change the form of the earth's substance by erosion.'' It is in this syntax that Gilbert and George's use of the term for their work may be most meaningfully grasped. Year after year they work not so much ''to change the form of the earth's substance'' as to erode our stubborn preconceptions about the earth's peoples and what it means to live an honorable life. It is the dominating commitment of their lives, as expressed through the medium of art. They often title their exhibitions, like the works, as clues to their artistic aspirations: *Modern Fears*, *Crusade*, *Modern Faith*. Their ambition does not permit modesty or privacy, but demands personal courage, dedicated vigilance, heartbreaking honesty, and admission of vulnerability. In the work of Gilbert and George, it is the unrelenting truth to life that invests their art with such conspicuous ethical significance. Taken as a whole, piece by piece, chapter by chapter, their work comprises a solemn scripture that inspires respect, riveted attention, and searing introspection.

Brenda Richardson

Notes

1. All quotes and paraphrases from Gilbert and George, cited throughout the text in quotation marks or explicitly referenced to the artists, derive from conversations with the author in London, May 10–15, September 19–22, and November 15–19, 1983. All section titles and extended quotations are drawn from published works by Gilbert and George, as follows: "No puzzle, just difficult truth," from *Side by Side* (London: Art for All, 1971), p. 37; "We are only human sculptors," from *Magazine Sculpture*, commissioned by *The Times*, London, 1970; "the most serious intentions in the world," from *A Message from the Sculptors*, 1970, and also *Walking*, 1970; "to do this funny thing," from the text to a three-panel charcoal on paper sculpture, *To Be With Art Is All We Ask*, 1970; "walking along a new road," from *A Message from the Sculptors*, 1970, and also *Walking*, 1970; "we are sometimes a little tired," from *A Guide to Singing Sculpture*, 1970; "there is a little more to the story," from *Magazine Sculpture*, 1970; "Is to become an artist," from the text to a three-panel charcoal on paper sculpture, *To Be With Art Is All We Ask*, 1970.
2. Greenaway, in telephone conversation with the author in London on November 19, 1983, reported that he has been familiar with the work of Gilbert and George since the late 1960's and remembers attending presentations of *The Singing Sculpture*. The filmmaker reports that he did not base his concept of the "living statues" in *The Draughtsman's Contract* on any specific historical precedent, but rather forged it from several different, more general sources. In particular, he was thinking of the role of "The Green Man," the bacchanal figure representing the spirit of nature, as represented in the poetry of Edmund Spenser and even before, or to the Shakespearean Puck or Fool figure, holding the rather privileged position granted the jester. More specifically, Greenaway reports that he based the film's "living statues" (which, in the original uncut version, included a wife and dog as "statues," along with the male figure which appears in the final film version) on two conceits: first, the late seventeenth-century vogue of the Grand Tour abroad for Englishmen, travel which often included the acquisition of Greek and Roman sculpture for English gardens; and, second, during the same period, the fashion in northern France for lead fountain statuary in gardens, with the figure statues designed to spout water from especially suggestive orifices (during garden parties, then, the host would arrange to have his gardener turn the fountains on unexpectedly and drench the guests). I am extremely grateful to Peter Greenaway for his generosity and warmth in discussing the concept of the "living statues" in his film, and its possible relationship to the work of Gilbert and George.

THE PHOTO-PIECES

MODERN FEARS, Anthony d'Offay Gallery, London, 1980.

MODERN FEARS, Anthony d'Offay Gallery, London, 1980.

PHOTO-PIECES 1971–1980, Stedelijk Van Abbemuseum Eindhoven, The Netherlands, 1980.

HAYWARD ANNUAL, London, 1979.

PHOTO-PIECES 1971–1980, Stedelijk Van Abbemuseum Eindhoven, The Netherlands, 1980.

PHOTO-PIECES 1971–1980, Stedelijk Van Abbemuseum Eindhoven, The Netherlands, 1980.

PHOTO-PIECES 1971–1980, Whitechapel Art Gallery, London, 1981.

PHOTO-PIECES 1971–1980, Whitechapel Art Gallery, London, 1981.

PHOTO-PIECES 1971–1980, Musée national d'art moderne, Centre Georges Pompidou, Paris, 1981.

PHOTO-PIECES 1971–1980, Musée national d'art moderne, Centre Georges Pompidou, Paris, 1981.

LIFE WITHOUT END and FINDING GOD, Gewad Gallery, Ghent, 1982.

PHOTO-PIECES 1971–1980, Kunsthalle Düsseldorf, 1981.

SAO PAULO BIENNALE, 1981.

GOOD NIGHT and FRIENDSHIP, "Zeitgeist," Berlin, 1982.

MODERN FAITH, Sonnabend Gallery, New York, 1983.

MODERN FAITH, Sonnabend Gallery, New York, 1983.

CHERRY BLOSSOM 12. 1974. 48 × 40¼ in. (122 × 102 cm.).
Collection of the artists.

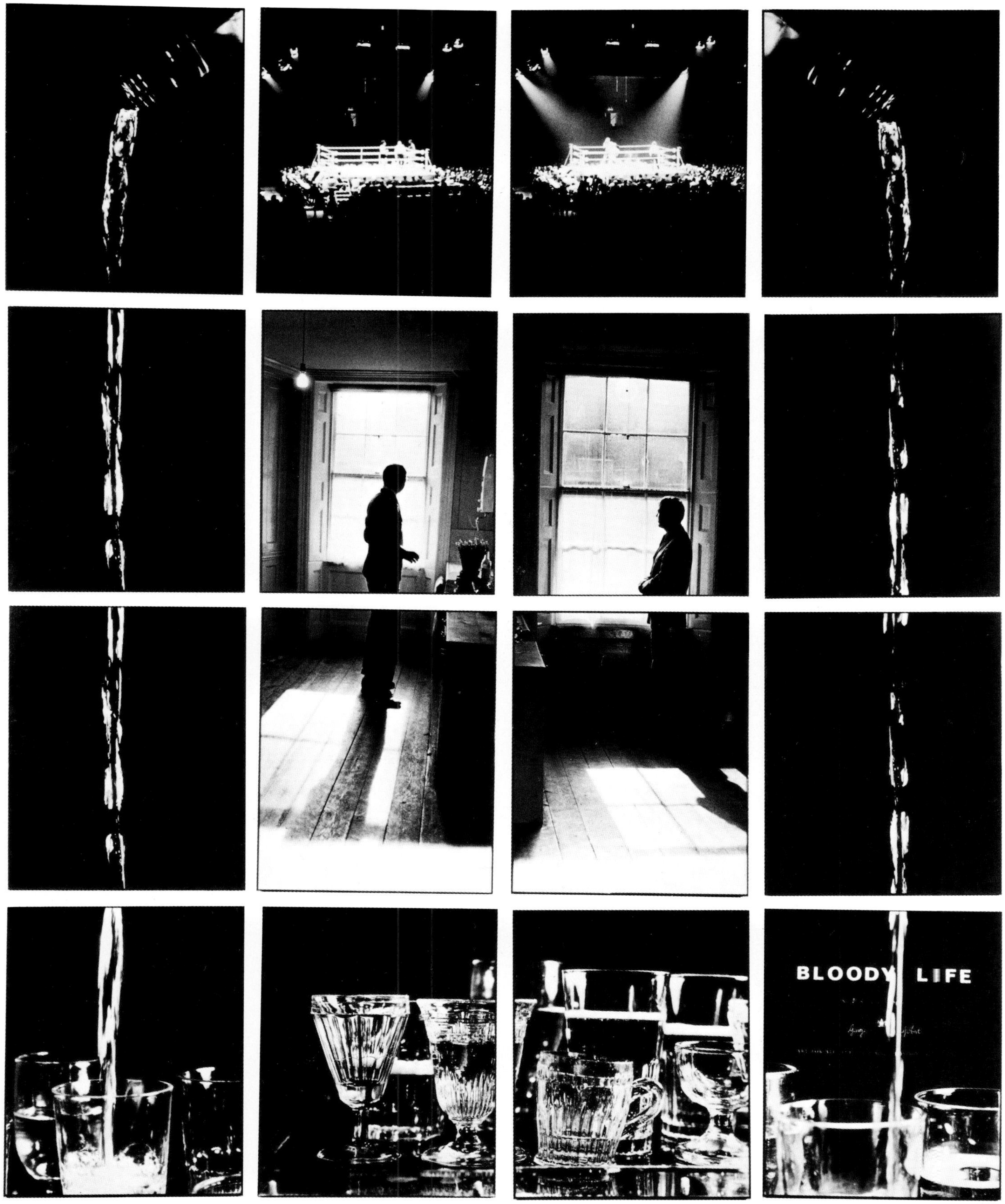

BLOODY LIFE 3. 1975. 96⅞ × 81⅛ in. (246 × 206 cm.).
Collection of Ileana and Michael Sonnabend, New York.

BAD THOUGHTS 7. 1975. 96⅞ × 81⅛ in. (246 × 206 cm.).
Collection of the artists.

DUSTY CORNERS 16. 1975. 48 × 40¼ in. (122 × 102 cm.).
Collection of William Burke, New York.

DEAD BOARDS 18. 1976. 48 × 40¼ in. (122 × 102 cm.).
Sonnabend Gallery, New York.

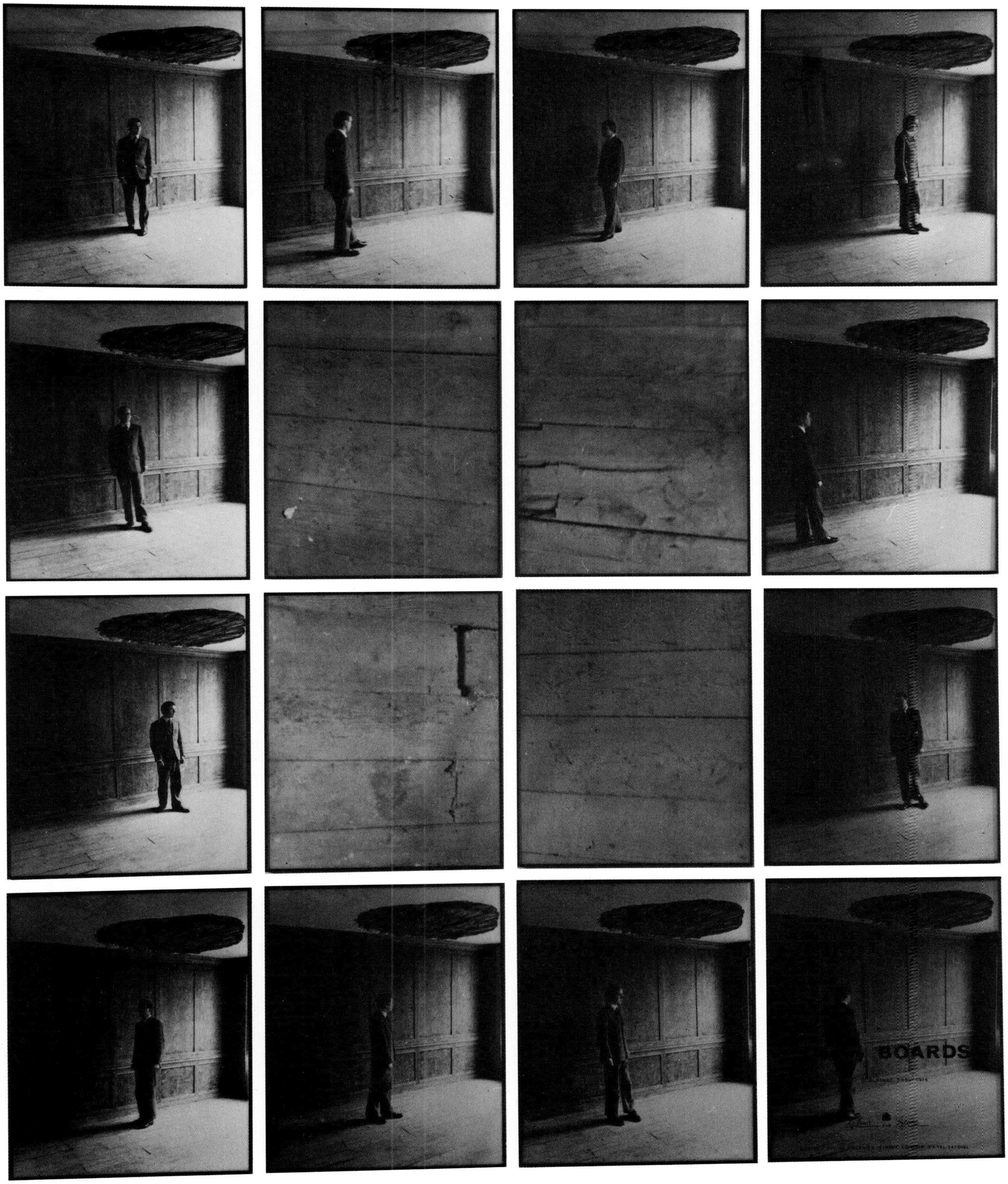

DEAD BOARDS 9. 1976. 96⅞ × 81⅛ in. (246 × 206 cm.).
Jedermann Collection, N.A.

MENTAL 2. 1976. 121¼ × 101⅝ in. (308 × 258 cm.).
Rijksmuseum Kröller-Müller, Otterlo, The Netherlands.

RED MORNING DEATH. 1977. 96 × 79 in. (242 × 200.8 cm.).
Art & Project, Amsterdam.

BENT. 1977. 95 × 79 in. (242 × 200.8 cm.).
Collection of Jan Dibbets, Amsterdam.

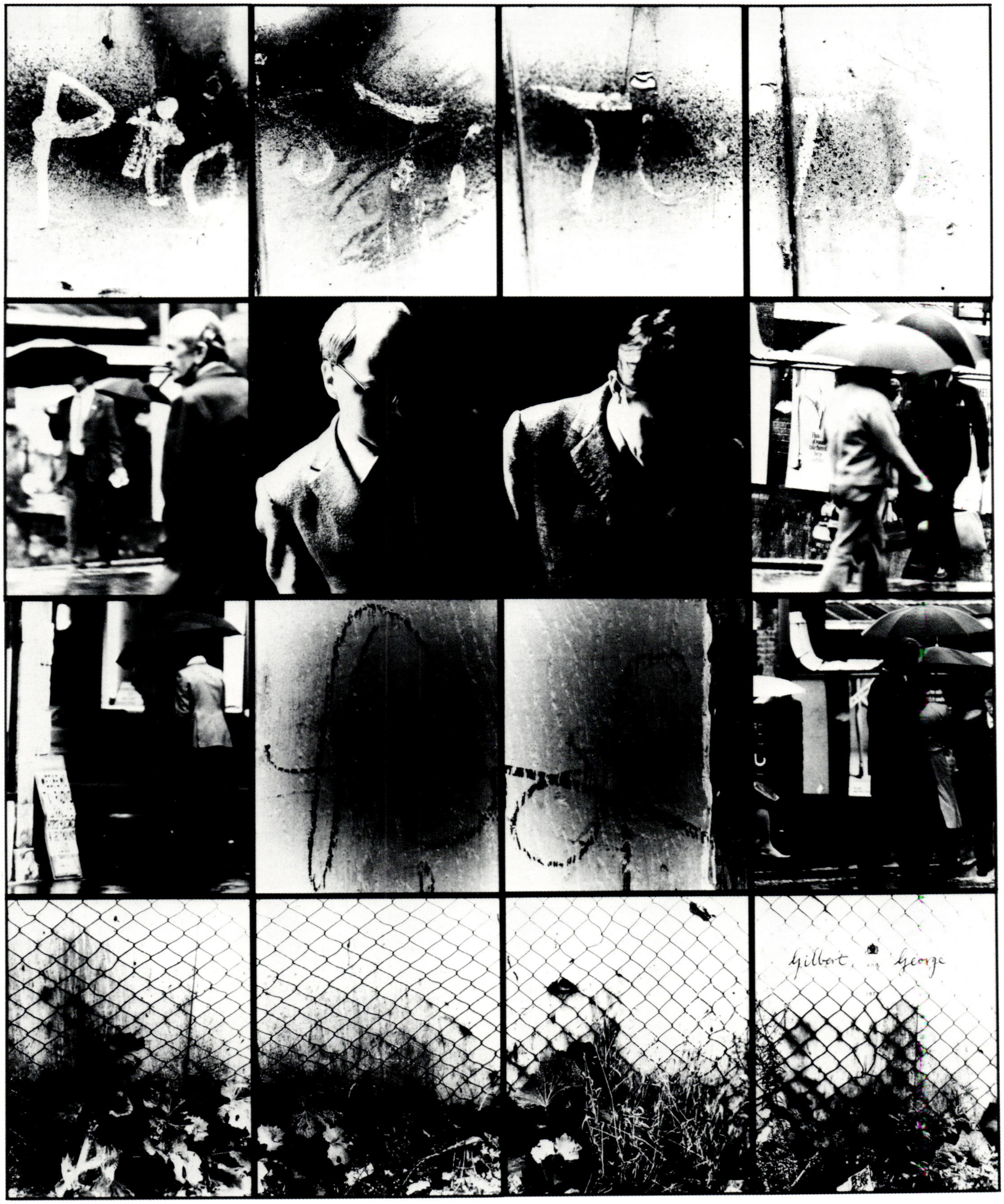

PROSTITUTE POOF. 1977. 95 × 79 in. (242 × 200.8 cm.).
Private Collection, Greenwich, Connecticut.

ARE YOU ANGRY OR ARE YOU BORING? 1977. 95 × 79 in. (242 × 200.8 cm.).
Stedelijk Van Abbemuseum Eindhoven, The Netherlands.

QUEER. 1977. 118¾ × 98¾ in. (302.5 × 251 cm.).
Museum Boymans-Van Beuningen, Rotterdam.

COMMUNISM. 1977. 118¾ × 98¾ in. (302.5 × 251 cm.).
Collection of Mr. and Mrs. Anton Herbert, Ghent, Belgium, courtesy Anthony d'Offay Gallery, London.

THE BRANCH. 1978. 95 × 79 in. (242 × 200.8 cm.).
Collection of Ealan J. Wingate, New York.

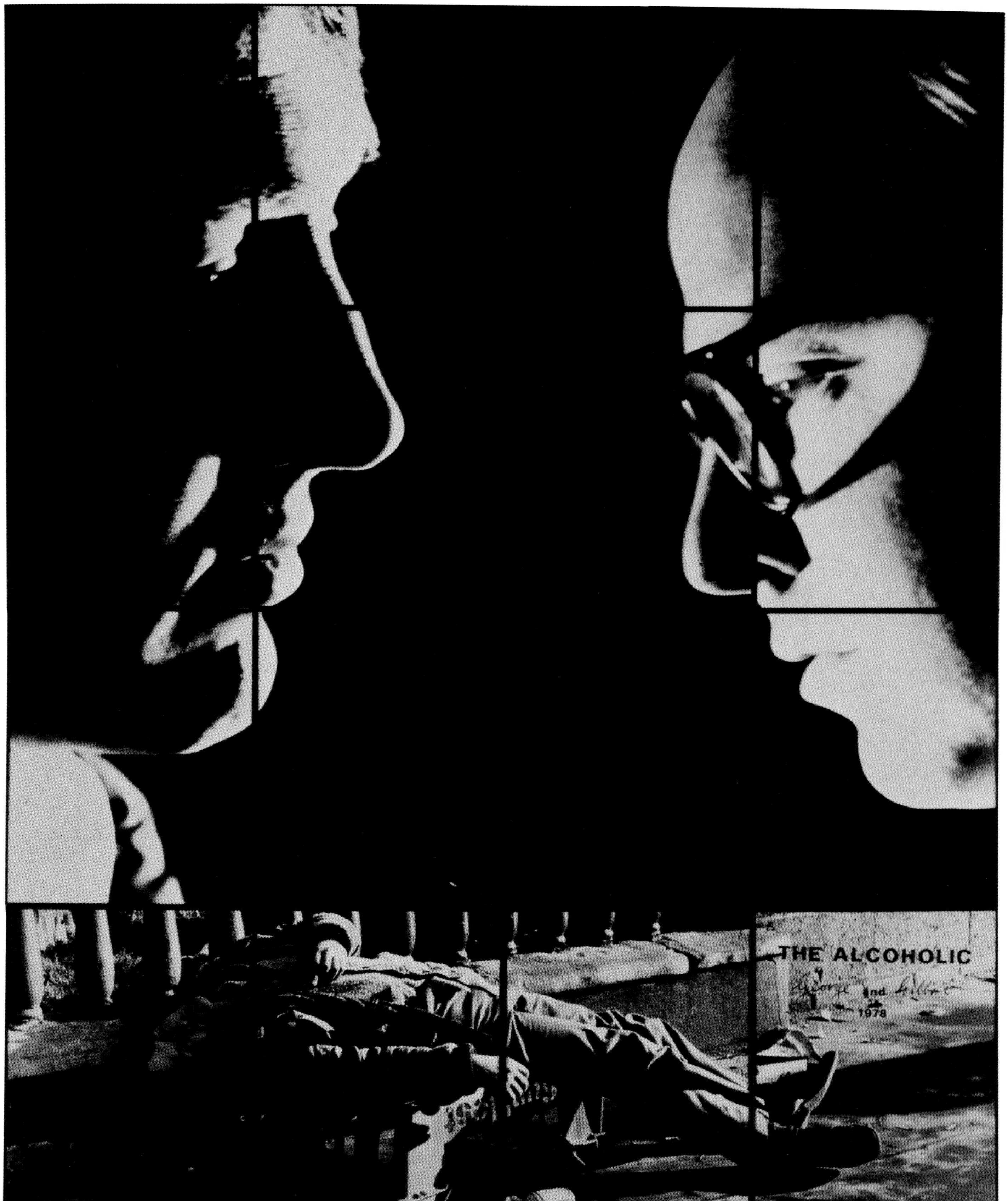

THE ALCOHOLIC. 1978. 95 × 79 in. (242 × 200.8 cm.).
The Art Institute of Chicago.

THE TREE. 1978. 95 × 79 in. (242 × 200.8 cm.).
The Sydney and Frances Lewis Foundation Collection.

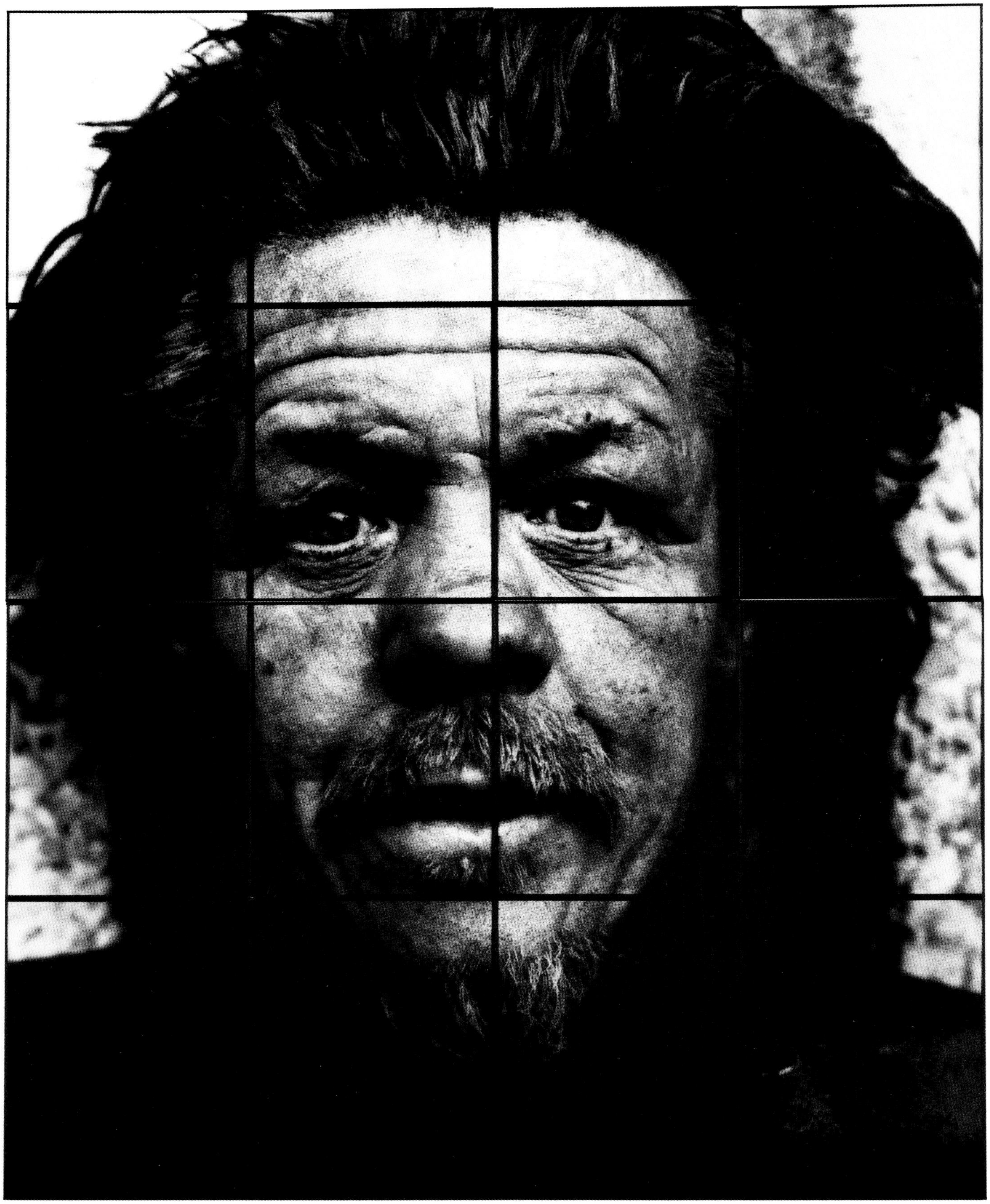

MAD. 1980. 95 × 79 in. (242 × 200.8 cm.).
Sonnabend Gallery, New York.

WAITING. 1980. 95 × 79 in. (242 × 200.8 cm.).
Private Collection, Baltimore.

FRUIT. 1980. 95 × 79 in. (242 × 200.8 cm.).
Collection of Charles B. Wright, Seattle.

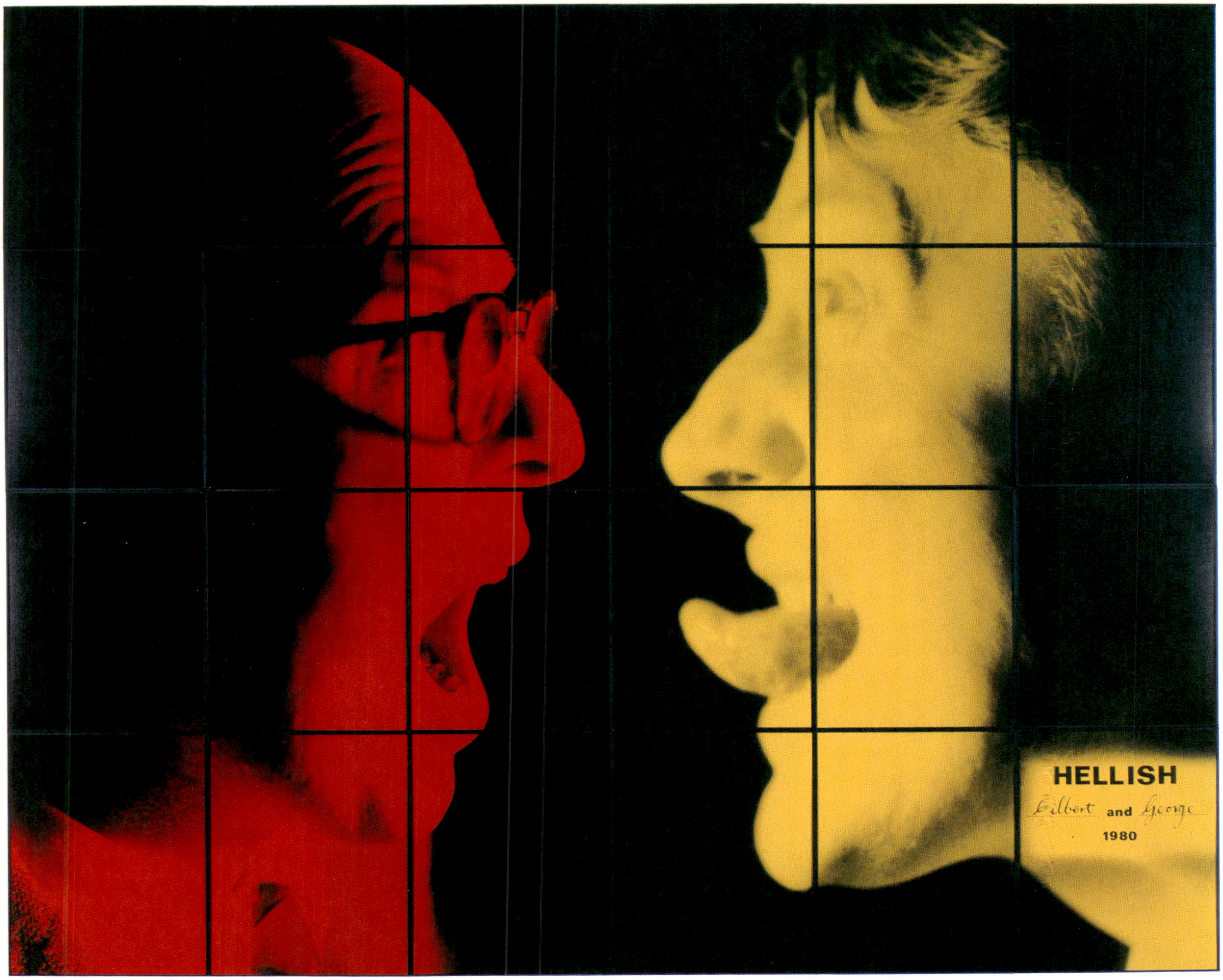

HELLISH. 1980. 95 × 118½ in. (242 × 301.2 cm.).
The Baltimore Museum of Art: Nelson and Juanita Greif Gutman Fund (BMA 1980.127).

UP. 1980. 95 × 79 in. (242 × 200.8 cm.).
Anthony d'Offay Gallery, London.

FIGHTER. 1980. 71¼ × 79 in. (181.5 × 200.8 cm.).
Anthony d'Offay Gallery, London.

MISERY. 1980. 95 × 158 in. (242 × 401.6 cm.).
Museum Boymans-Van Beuningen, Rotterdam.

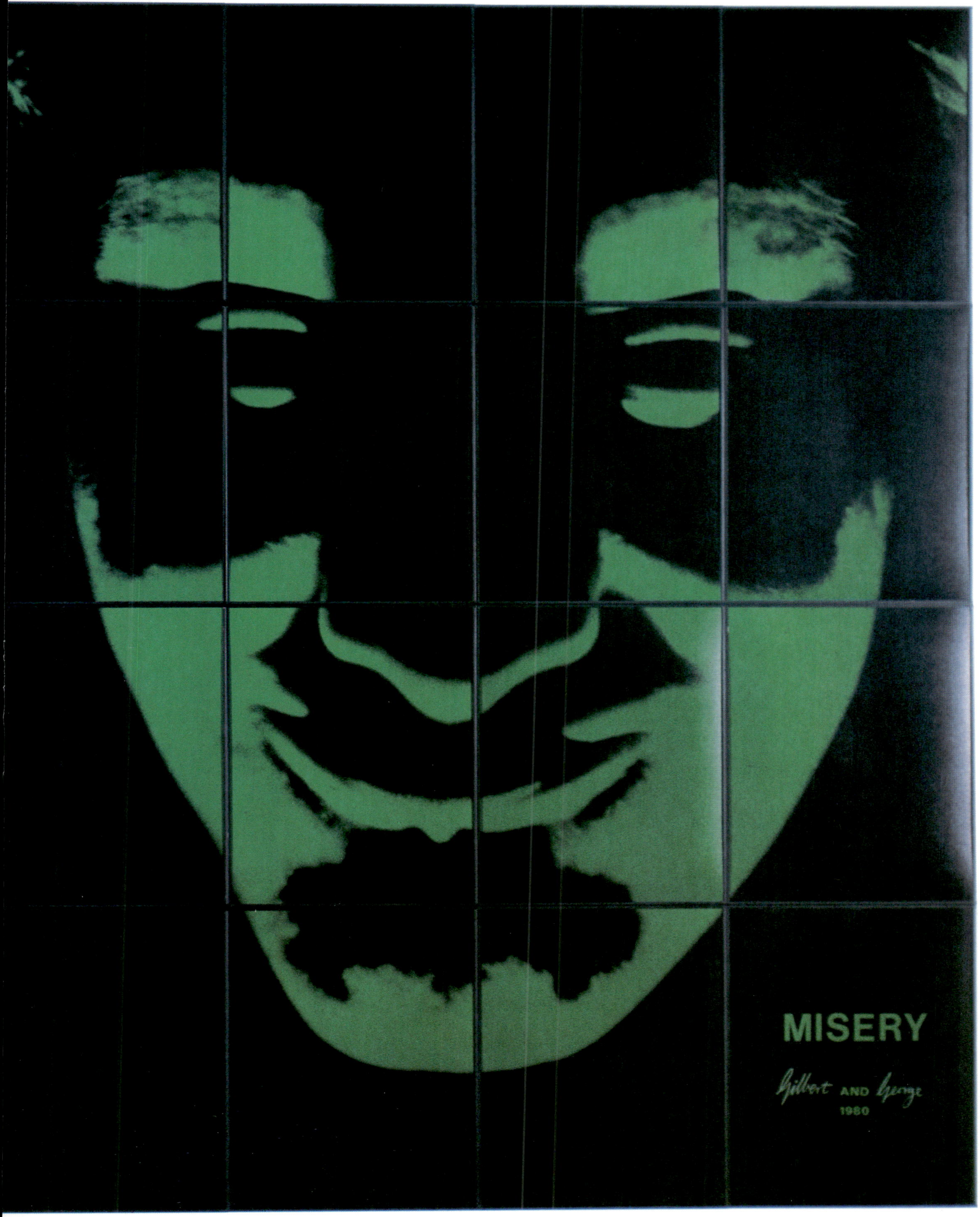
MISERY
Gilbert AND George
1980

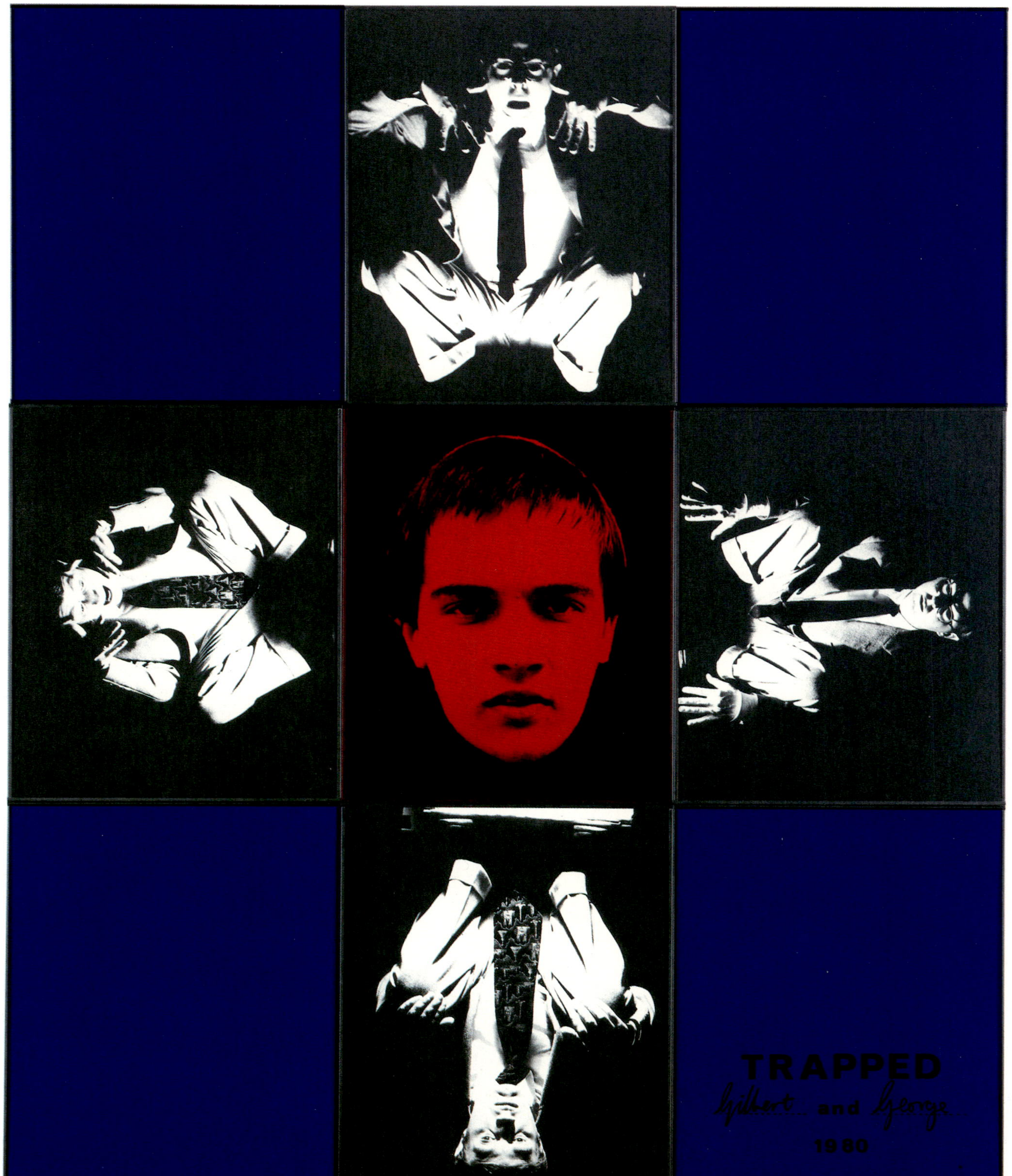

TRAPPED. 1980. 71¼ × 59¼ in. (181.5 × 150.6 cm.).
Private Collection, Baltimore.

EXHAUSTED. 1980. 95 × 79 in. (242 × 200.8 cm.).
Scottish National Gallery of Modern Art, Edinburgh.

FOUR KNIGHTS. 1980. 95 × 79 in. (242 × 200.8 cm.).
Southampton Art Gallery, England.

FOUR FEELINGS. 1980. 95 × 79 in. (242 × 200.8 cm.).
Private Collection, New York.

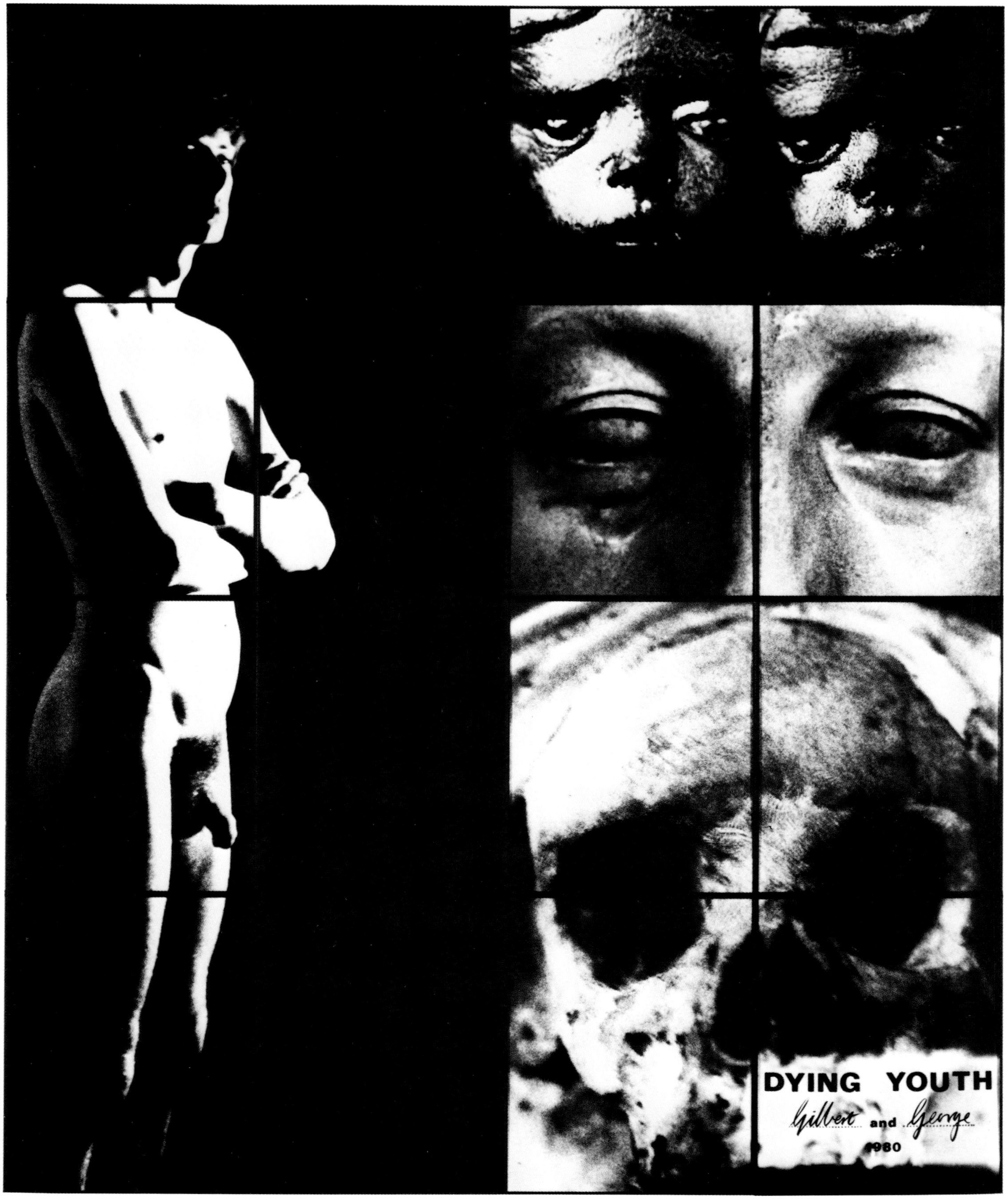

DYING YOUTH. 1980. 95 × 79 in. (242 × 200.8 cm.).
Collection of Lucio Amelio, Naples, Italy.

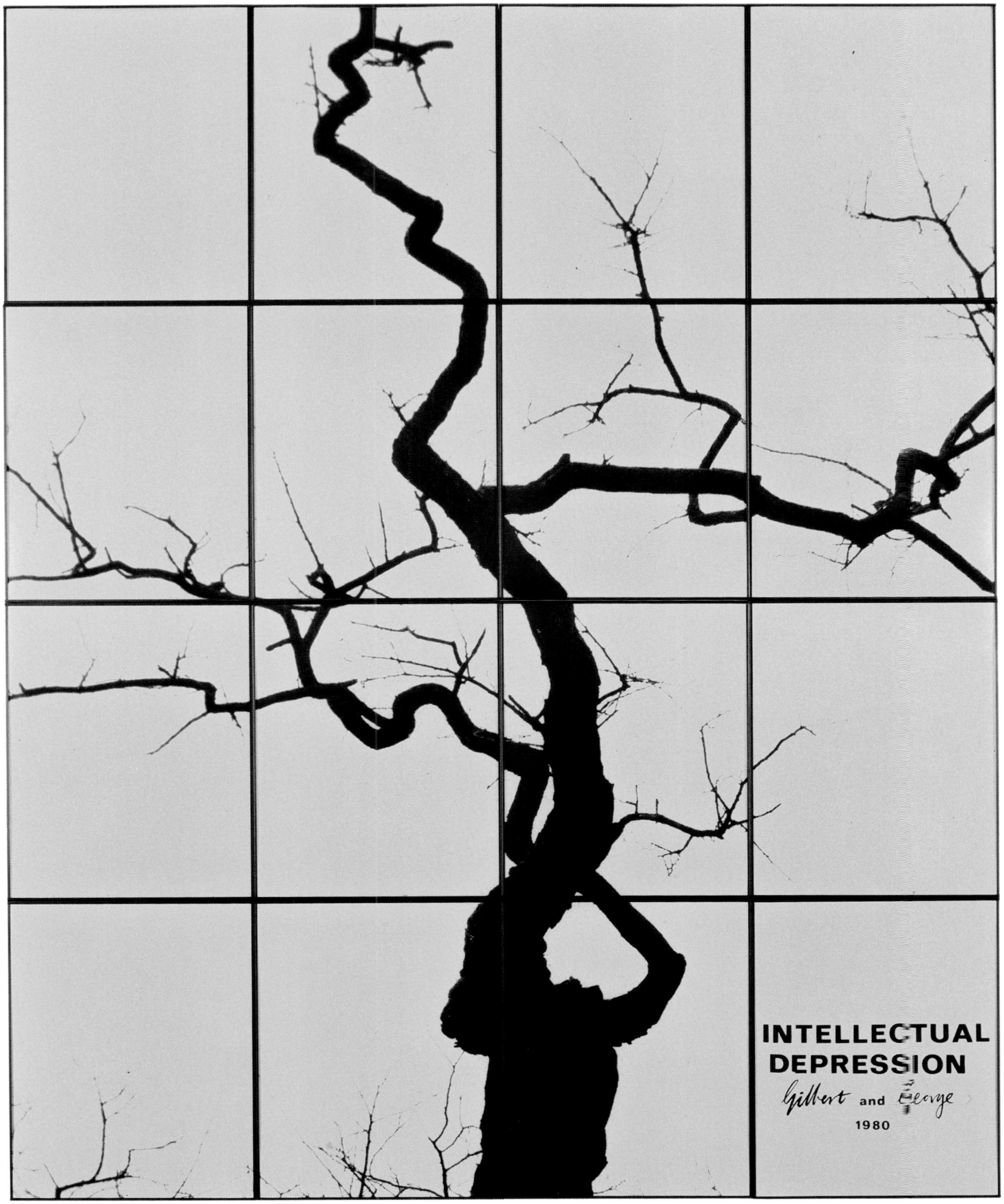

INTELLECTUAL DEPRESSION. 1980. 95 × 79 in. (242 × 200.8 cm.).
The British Council.

BLACK CHURCH FACE. 1980. 95 × 79 in. (242 × 200.8 cm.).
Collection of Michael Sonnabend, New York.

FALLEN LEAVES. 1980. 95 × 79 in. (242 × 200.8 cm.).
Anthony d'Offay Gallery, London.

ANGELS. 1980. 95 × 118½ in. (242 × 301.2 cm.).
Collection of Mr. and Mrs. Ronald F. Ostrow, New York.

HERO. 1980. 71¼ × 118½ in. (181.5 × 301.2 cm.).
Collection of Massimo and Francesca Valsecchi, Milan and London.

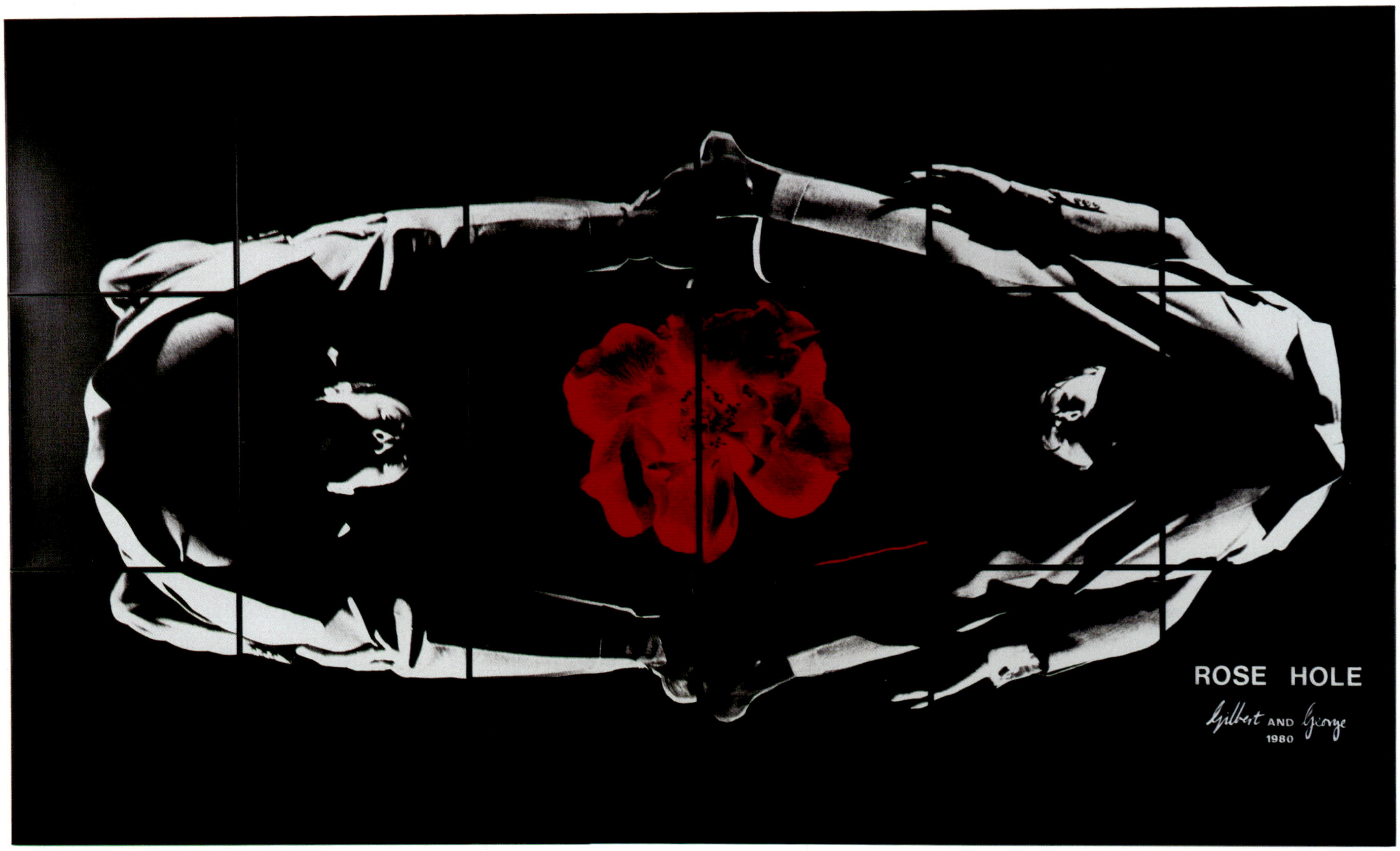

ROSE HOLE. 1980. 71¼ × 118½ in. (181.5 × 301.2 cm.).
Sanders Collection, Amsterdam.

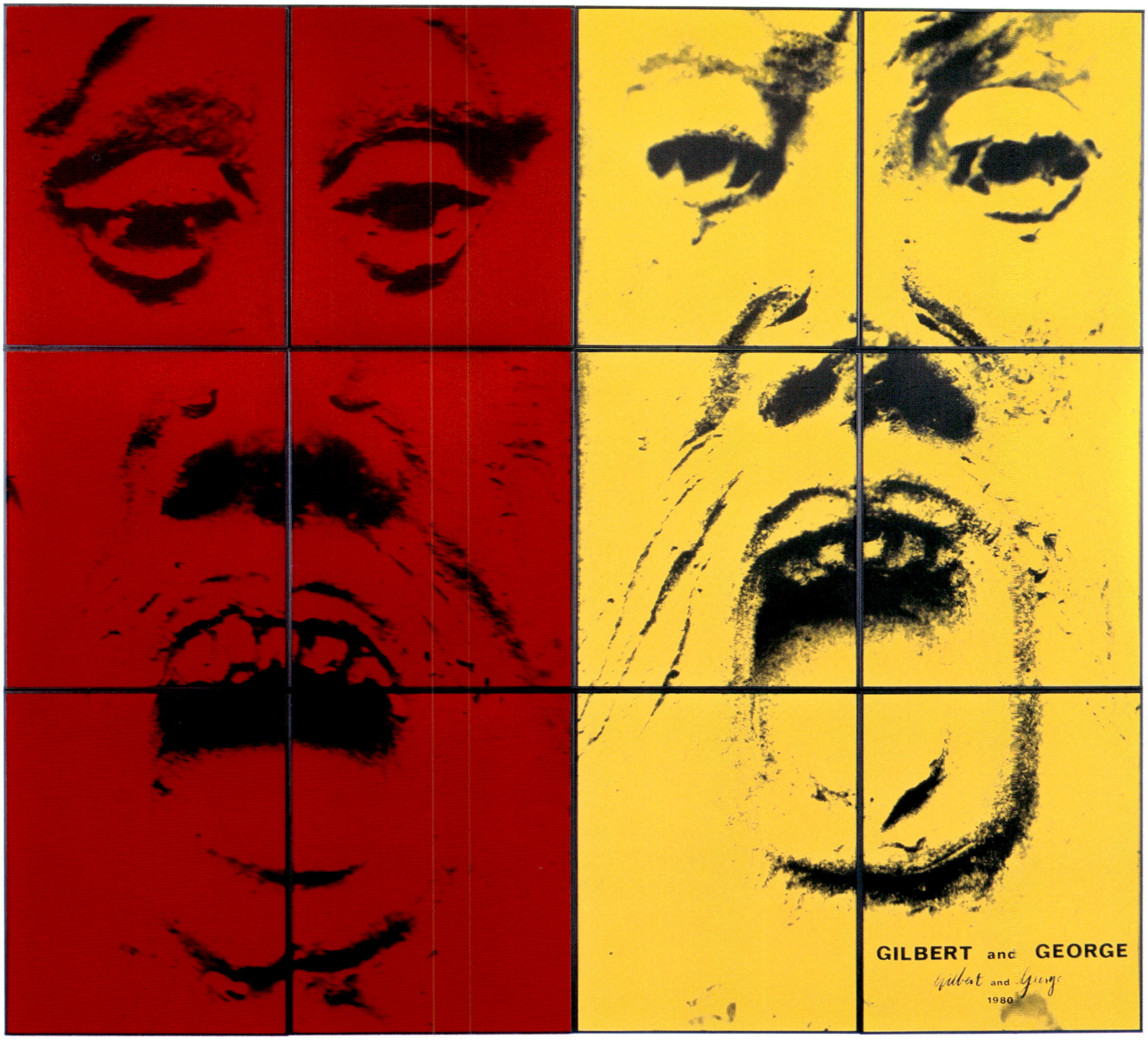

GILBERT AND GEORGE. 1980. 71¼ × 79 in. (181.5 × 200.8 cm.).
Collection of Ealan J. Wingate, New York.

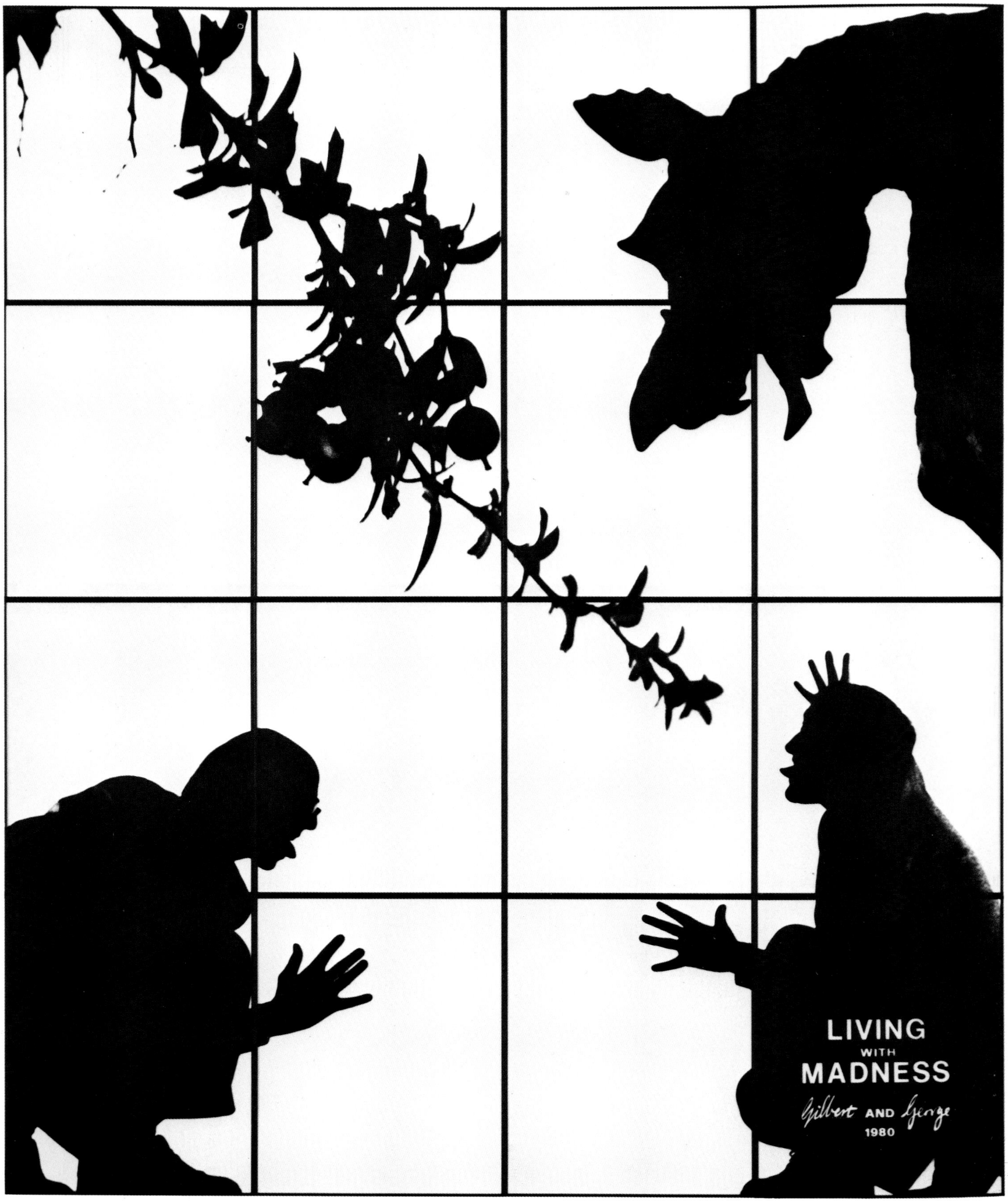

LIVING WITH MADNESS. 1980. 95 × 79 in. (242 × 200.8 cm.).
Collection of Ealan J. Wingate, New York.

BLACK DAY. 1980. 95 × 79 in. (242 × 200.8 cm.).
Anthony d'Offay Gallery, London.

LIONS. 1980. 47½ × 39½ in. (121 × 100.4 cm.).
Collection of Clarissa Dalrymple, New York.

COLOURED FAITH. 1980. 47½ × 39½ in. (121 × 100.4 cm.).
Private Collection, London.

MONSTER. 1980. 47½ × 39½ in. (121 × 100.4 cm.).
Galerie Crousel-Hussenot, Paris.

COLOURED BLACK. 1981. 47½ × 39½ in. (121 × 100.4 cm.).
Collection of Anthony Collett and Julia Pines, London.

RUDE. 1981. 95 × 79 in. (242 × 200.8 cm.).
Galerie Crousel-Hussenot, Paris.

SPEAKING YOUTH. 1981. 95 × 79 in. (242 × 200.8 cm.).
Collection of Joan Sonnabend, Boston.

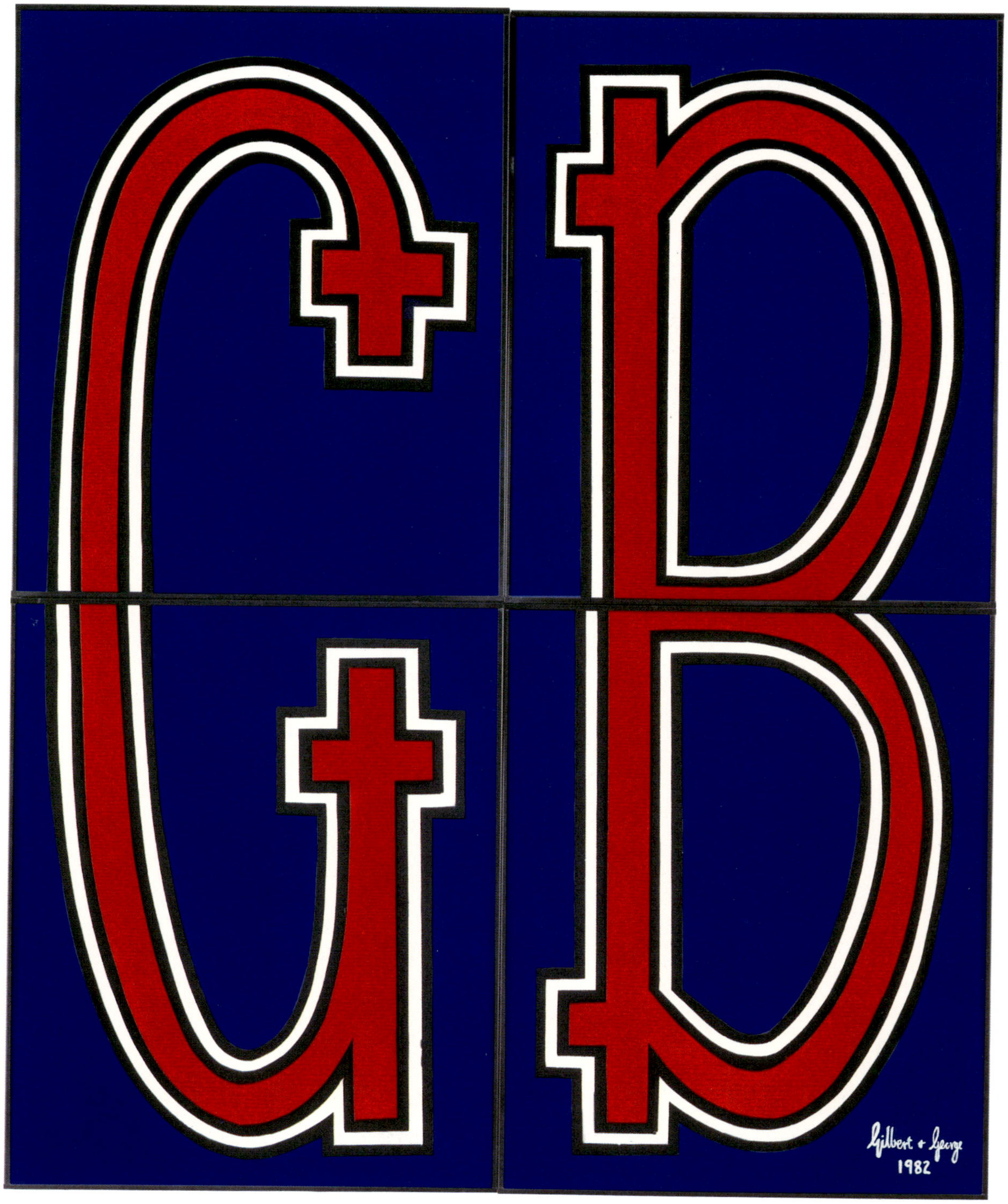

G B. 1982. 47½ × 39½ in. (121 × 100.4 cm.).
Galerie Crousel-Hussenot, Paris.

DEATHO KNOCKO. 1982. 166¼ × 158 in. (423.5 × 401.6 cm.).
Anthony d'Offay Gallery, London.

NAKED LOVE. 1982. 118¾ × 118½ in. (302.5 × 301.2 cm.).
Anthony d'Offay Gallery, London.

YOUTH FAITH. 1982. 118¾ × 118½ in. (302.5 × 301.2 cm.).
Collection of Andrew Colls, London.

LIFE HORROR. 1982. 71¼ × 79 in. (181.5 × 200.8 cm.).
The Norton Gallery of Art, West Palm Beach, Florida.

VARIOUS LOVES. 1982. 71¼ × 79 in. (181.5 × 200.8 cm.).
Collection of Ealan J. Wingate, New York.

COLOURED LOVES. 1982. 95 × 98¾ in. (242 × 251 cm.).
Private Collection, New York.

WINTER FLOWERS. 1982. 95 × 98¾ in. (242 × 251 cm.).
Collection of Arthur and Carol Goldberg, New York.

LOVE LAKE. 1982. 95 × 79 in. (242 × 200.8 cm.).
Collection of Irwin Joffe, London.

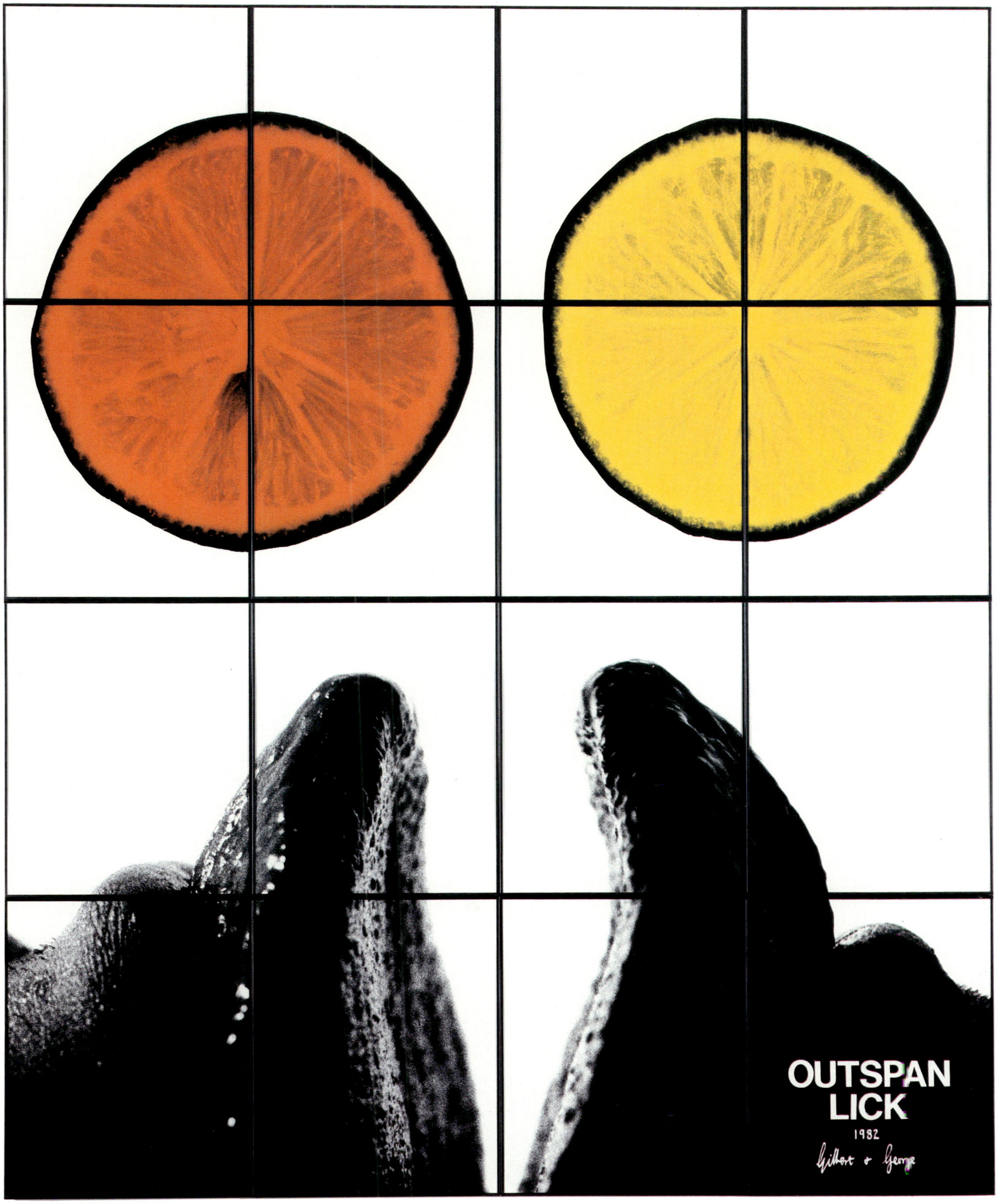

OUTSPAN LICK. 1982. 95 × 79 in. (242 × 200.8 cm.).
Sonnabend Gallery, New York.

LICKERS. 1982. 95 × 79 in. (242 × 200.8 cm.).
Anthony d'Offay Gallery, London.

NIGHT CRUSADE. 1982. 71¼ × 98¾ in. (181.5 × 251 cm.).
Sonnabend Gallery, New York.

NAKED BEAUTY. 1982. 71¼ × 98¾ in. (181.5 × 251 cm.).
Collection of Sherry and William Fabrikant, King's Point, New York.

FROZEN YOUTH. 1982. 95 × 118½ in. (242 × 301.2 cm.).
Collection of Gerald S. Elliott, Chicago.

SEVEN HEROES. 1982. 71¼ × 138¼ in. (181.5 × 351.4 cm.).
Collection of Ileana and Michael Sonnabend, New York.

FORGIVENESS. 1982. 95 × 79 in. (242 × 200.8 cm.).
Sonnabend Gallery, New York.

PINK PRINCE. 1983. 95 × 79 in. (242 × 200.8 cm.).
Collection of Anne and Anthony d'Offay, London.

DAY AND NIGHT. 1982. 95 × 118½ in. (242 × 301.2 cm.).
Anthony d'Offay Gallery, London.

FRUIT GOD FEAR. 1982. 118¾ × 98¾ in. (302.5 × 251 cm.).
Sonnabend Gallery, New York.

URINIGHT. 1982. 118¾ × 118½ in. (302.5 × 301.2 cm.).
Sonnabend Gallery, New York.

LIFE WITHOUT END. 1982. 166¼ × 434½ in. (423.5 × 1104.4 cm.).
Sonnabend Gallery, New York.

LIFE
WITHOUT
END

34. UP. 1980. Black-and-white photographs, mounted and framed, 16-part. 95 x 79 in. (242 x 200.8 cm.). Anthony d'Offay Gallery, London.

35. WAITING. 1980. Black-and-white photographs, dyed yellow, mounted and framed, 16-part. 95 x 79 in. (242 x 200.8 cm.). Private Collection, Baltimore.

36. HERO. 1980. Black-and-white photographs, nine dyed yellow, mounted and framed, 18-part. 71¼ x 118½ in. (181.5 x 301.2 cm.). Collection of Massimo and Francesca Valsecchi, Milan and London.

37. ROSE HOLE. 1980. Black-and-white photographs, two dyed red, mounted and framed, 18-part. 71¼ x 118½ in. (181.5 x 301.2 cm.). Sanders Collection, Amsterdam.

38. ANGELS. 1980. Black-and-white photographs, dyed yellow, mounted and framed, 24-part. 95 x 118½ in. (242 x 301.2 cm.). Collection of Mr. and Mrs. Ronald F. Ostrow, New York.

39. HELLISH. 1980. Black-and-white photographs, twelve dyed red and twelve dyed yellow, mounted and framed, 24-part. 95 x 118½ in. (242 x 301.2 cm.). The Baltimore Museum of Art: Nelson and Juanita Greif Gutman Fund (BMA 1980.127).

40. MISERY. 1980. Black-and-white photographs, dyed green, mounted and framed, 32-part. 95 x 158 in. (242 x 401.6 cm.). Museum Boymans-Van Beuningen, Rotterdam.

41. COLOURED BLACK. 1981. Black-and-white photograms, one each dyed red, green, blue, and yellow, mounted and framed, 4-part. 47½ x 39½ in. (121 x 100.4 cm.). Collection of Anthony Collett and Julia Pines, London.

42. RUDE. 1981. Black-and-white photograms, eight dyed blue and eight dyed orange, mounted and framed, 16-part. 95 x 79 in. (242 x 200.8 cm.). Galerie Crousel-Hussenot, Paris.

43. SPEAKING YOUTH. 1981. Black-and-white photograms, dyed yellow, mounted and framed, 16-part. 95 x 79 in. (242 x 200.8 cm.). Collection of Joan Sonnabend, Boston.

44. GB. 1982. Black-and-white photograms, hand-colored in red and blue, mounted and framed, 4-part. 47½ x 39½ in. (121 x 100.4 cm.). Galerie Crousel-Hussenot, Paris.

45. LIFE HORROR. 1982. Black-and-white photographs and photograms, hand-colored in red, with gold leaf, mounted and framed, 12-part. 71¼ x 79 in. (181.5 x 200.8 cm.). The Norton Gallery of Art, West Palm Beach, Florida.

46. VARIOUS LOVES. 1982. Black-and-white photographs, hand-colored in pink, yellow, and blue, mounted and framed, 12-part. 71¼ x 79 in. (181.5 x 200.8 cm.). Collection of Ealan J. Wingate, New York.

47. NAKED BEAUTY. 1982. Black-and-white photographs, hand-colored in pink and yellow, with gold leaf, mounted and framed, 15-part. 71¼ x 98¾ in. (181.5 x 251 cm.). Collection of Sherry and William Fabrikant, King's Point, New York.

48. NIGHT CRUSADE. 1982. Black-and-white photographs and photograms, hand-colored in red, mounted and framed, 15-part. 71¼ x 98¾ in. (181.5 x 251 cm.). Sonnabend Gallery, New York.

49. FORGIVENESS. 1982. Black-and-white photographs and photograms, hand-colored in pink, yellow, and blue, with gold leaf, mounted and framed, 16-part. 95 x 79 in. (242 x 200.8 cm.). Sonnabend Gallery, New York.

50. LICKERS. 1982. Black-and-white photograms, hand-colored in red, mounted and framed, 16-part. 95 x 79 in. (242 x 200.8 cm.). Anthony d'Offay Gallery, London.

51. LOVE LAKE. 1982. Black-and-white photograms, hand-colored in red, blue, yellow, and green, mounted and framed, 16-part. 95 x 79 in. (242 x 200.8 cm.). Collection of Irwin Joffe, London.

52. OUTSPAN LICK. 1982. Black-and-white photographs, hand-colored in orange and yellow, mounted and framed, 16-part. 95 x 79 in. (242 x 200.8 cm.). Sonnabend Gallery, New York.

53. COLOURED LOVES. 1982. Black-and-white photographs, hand-colored in orange, blue, yellow, and pink, mounted and framed, 20-part. 95 x 98¾ in. (242 x 251 cm.). Private Collection, New York.

54. WINTER FLOWERS. 1982. Black-and-white photographs, hand-colored in red, yellow, blue, and violet, mounted and framed, 20-part. 95 x 98¾ in. (242 x 251 cm.). Collection of Arthur and Carol Goldberg, New York.

55. SEVEN HEROES. 1982. Black-and-white photographs, hand-colored in red, blue, yellow, and green, with gold leaf, mounted and framed, 21-part. 71¼ x 138¼ in. (181.5 x 351.4 cm.). Collection of Ileana and Michael Sonnabend, New York.

56. DAY AND NIGHT. 1982. Black-and-white photographs and photograms, hand-colored in yellow, orange, green, pink, and blue, with gold leaf, mounted and framed, 24-part. 95 x 118½ in. (242 x 301.2 cm.). Anthony d'Offay Gallery, London.

57. FROZEN YOUTH. 1982. Black-and-white photographs, hand-colored in red, yellow, and blue, mounted and framed, 24-part. 95 x 118½ in. (242 x 301.2 cm.). Collection of Gerald S. Elliott, Chicago.

58. FRUIT GOD FEAR. 1982. Black-and-white photographs, hand-colored in red, yellow, blue, green, and orange, mounted and framed, 25-part. 118¾ x 98¾ in. (302.5 x 251 cm.). Sonnabend Gallery, New York.

59. NAKED LOVE. 1982. Black-and-white photographs, hand-colored in pink, mounted and framed, 30-part. 118¾ x 118½ in. (302.5 x 301.2 cm.). Anthony d'Offay Gallery, London.

60. URINIGHT. 1982. Black-and-white photographs, hand-colored in yellow and blue, mounted and framed, 30-part. 118¾ x 118½ in. (302.5 x 301.2 cm.). Sonnabend Gallery, New York.

61. YOUTH FAITH. 1982. Black-and-white photographs and photograms, hand-colored in red, yellow, blue, green, orange, pink, and violet, mounted and framed, 30-part. 118¾ x 118½ in. (302.5 x 301.2 cm.). Collection of Andrew Colls, London.

62. DEATHO KNOCKO. 1982. Black-and-white photographs, mounted and framed, 56-part. 166¼ x 158 in. (423.5 x 401.6 cm.). Anthony d'Offay Gallery, London.

63. LIFE WITHOUT END. 1982. Black-and-white photographs and photograms, hand-colored in red, yellow, blue, green, orange, pink, and violet, mounted and framed, 154-part. 166¼ x 434½ in. (423.5 x 1104.4 cm.). Sonnabend Gallery, New York.

64. PINK PRINCE. 1983. Black-and-white photographs and photograms, hand-colored in red, pink, orange, and blue, with gold leaf, mounted and framed, 16-part. 95 x 79 in. (242 x 200.8 cm.). Collection of Anne and Anthony d'Offay, London.

Catalogue numbers 65, 66, and 67, all created especially for the Baltimore exhibition, were in progress at the time of publication. All three of these photo-pieces were loaned to the exhibition through the courtesy of the Anthony d'Offay Gallery, London, and the Sonnabend Gallery, New York.

65. DRAINED. 1983. Black-and-white photographs and photograms, hand-colored, mounted and framed, 24-part. 95 x 118½ in. (242 x 301.2 cm.).

66. WORLD. 1983. Black-and-white photographs, hand-colored, mounted and framed, 24-part. 95 x 118½ in. (242 x 301.2 cm.).

67. YOUNG. 1983. Black-and-white photographs and photograms, hand-colored, mounted and framed, 24-part. 95 x 118½ in. (242 x 301.2 cm.).

BIOGRAPHY

The following documentation was compiled by Gilbert and George, with the assistance of Judy Adam of the Anthony d'Offay Gallery, London. Bibliographic items are cited in chronological rather than alphabetical order. Entries have not been independently verified.

GILBERT	GEORGE
Born Dolomites, Italy, 1943	Born Devon, England, 1942

Studied

Wolkenstein School of Art	Dartington Adult Education Centre
Hallein School of Art	Dartington Hall College of Art
Munich Academy of Art	Oxford School of Art

Met and Studied

St. Martin's School of Art, London, 1967

Publications

THE PENCIL ON PAPER DESCRIPTIVE WORKS (edition 500), published by Gilbert & George, London, 1970
ART NOTES AND THOUGHTS, published by Gilbert & George, London, 1970
TO BE WITH ART IS ALL WE ASK (edition 300), published by Gilbert & George, London, 1970
A GUIDE TO THE SINGING SCULPTURE, published by Gilbert & George, London, 1970
THE PAINTINGS, published by Kunstverein, Düsseldorf, 1971
SIDE BY SIDE (edition 600), published by König Bros., Cologne, 1971
A DAY IN THE LIFE OF GEORGE & GILBERT (edition 1,000), published by Gilbert & George, London, 1971
THE GRAND OLD DUKE OF YORK, published by Kunstmuseum, Lucerne, 1972
CATALOGUE FOR THEIR AUSTRALIAN VISIT, published by John Kaldor, Sydney, 1973
DARK SHADOW (edition 2,000), published by Nigel Greenwood, London, 1976
GILBERT & GEORGE, published by Taxispalais Gallery, Innsbruck, 1977

Postal sculptures

THE EASTER CARDS, 1969
SOUVENIR HYDE PARK WALK, 1969
A MESSAGE FROM THE SCULPTORS, 1969 (dated 1970)
ALL MY LIFE, 1969
NEW DECADENT ART, 1969/1970
THE SADNESS IN OUR ART, 1970
THE LIMERICKS, 1971
1ST POST-CARD, 1972
2ND POST-CARD, 1972
THE PINK ELEPHANTS, 1973
THE RED BOXERS, 1975

Magazine sculptures

THE WORDS OF THE SCULPTORS, *Jam Magazine*, Autumn 1969, pp. 43–47
THE SHIT AND THE CUNT, *Studio International*, May 1970, pp. 218–221
WITH US IN NATURE, Kunstmarkt, Cologne (Catalogue), 1970
TWO TEXT PAGES DESCRIBING OUR POSITION, *The Sunday Times Magazine*, January 10, 1971
THERE WERE TWO YOUNG MEN, *Studio International*, May 1971, pp. 220–221
BALLS, *Avalanche*, Summer-Fall 1973, pp. 26–33

Works in edition

THE WORDS OF THE SCULPTORS (edition 35), 1970
WALKING VIEWING RELAXING (edition 13), 1970
TO BE WITH ART IS ALL WE ASK (edition 9), 1970
TWO TEXT PAGES DESCRIBING OUR POSITION (edition 19), 1970
THE TEN SPEECHES (edition 10), 1971
THE EIGHT LIMERICKS (edition 25), 1971
MORNING LIGHT ON ART FOR ALL (edition 12), 1972
GREAT EXPECTATIONS (edition 12), 1972
AS USED BY THE SCULPTORS (edition 30), 1972
RECLINING DRUNK (edition 200), 1973
THE RED SCULPTURE ALBUM (edition 100), 1976
FIRST BLOSSOM (edition 50), 1979

Films and video

THE NATURE OF OUR LOOKING (edition 4), 1970
GORDON'S MAKES US DRUNK (edition 25), 1972
IN THE BUSH (edition 25), 1972
PORTRAIT OF THE ARTISTS AS YOUNG MEN (edition 25), 1972
THE WORLD OF GILBERT & GEORGE, produced by Philip Haas for the Arts Council of Great Britain (70 minutes), 1981

SELECTED BIBLIOGRAPHY

Ger van Elk, "We would honestly like to say how happy we are to be Sculptors," *Museumjournaal*, October 1969, pp. 248–249.

Caroline Tisdall, "Gilbert and George," *The Guardian*, November 20, 1970.

"Singende Skulptur-Glückliche Hauer," *Der Spiegel*, vol. 24, no. 45, 1970.

Carel Blotkamp, "De werken van Gilbert & George, soms in levende lijve," *Vrij Nederland*, June 13, 1970.

Francis Wyndham, "Gilbert and George," *Sunday Times*, January 10, 1971.

John Perreault, "Nothing breathtaking will occur here but . . . ," *Village Voice*, October 7, 1971.

Andrew Forge, "The paintings of John Hoyland & The sculpture of G & G," *The Listener*, July 22, 1971.

Barbara Reise, "Presenting Gilbert & George," *Art News*, November 1971, pp. 62–65.

Betty van Garrel, "Kunst als een vorm van leven," *Haages Post*, November 10, 1971, pp. 88–91.

"Gilbert and George," *The New Yorker*, October 9, 1971.

Donald Zec, "The odd couple," *Daily Mirror*, September 5, 1972.

Anne Seymour, "An interview," *The New Art* (exhibition catalogue), Hayward Gallery/Arts Council, London, 1972, pp. 92–95.

Richard Cork, "It's G & G, always the life & soul of the party," *Evening Standard*, July 22, 1972.

Karl Buhlmann, "Selbtsdarstellung als Bildsprache," *Luzerner Neueste Nachrichte*, May 25, 1972.

Caroline Tisdall, "The greatest two-man vaudeville act in the art galleries," *The Guardian*, November 30, 1972.

Richard Cork, "Make mine a double sculpture," *Evening Standard*, December 1, 1972.

Peter Weiermair, "Gilbert stammt aus dem Grodental," *Tiroler Tageszeitung*, January 15, 1972.

Germano Celant, "Gilbert & George," *Domus*, March 1972, pp. 50–53.

Chris Hector, "They keep stiff for hours," *Nation Review*, August 31, 1973.

Donald Brook, "Blur between art & life," *Nation Review*, August 31, 1973.

Michael Baudson, "Gilbert & George," *Clés pour les arts*, October 1973, p. 13.

Schuldt, "L'Angelus de Milo," *Art Vivant*, December 1973, pp. 9–11.

Carel Blotkamp, "Gilbert & George: on cooperation, on tradition," *Album Amicorum J. G. van Gelder*, The Hague, Nijhoff, 1973, pp. 42–46.

Daniel Thomas, "Still life on a table," *Sydney Morning Herald*, August 16, 1973.

Bruce Adams, "Gilbert & George for high tea," *Sunday Telegraph* (Sydney), August 26, 1973.

Leonore Nicklin, "And here come the living sculptures," *Sydney Morning Herald*, August 14, 1973.

Douglas Davis, "Living statues," *Newsweek*, December 3, 1973.

Tomaso Trini, "Gilbert & George the human sculptors," *Data*, Summer 1974, pp. 20–27.

Robert Novak, "Singing monuments," *Farrago Literary Supplement*, September 7, 1974.

"Gay Gordons," *Times Literary Supplement*, June 21, 1974.

Lynda Morris, "Gilbert and George," *Studio International*, July/August 1974, pp. 49–50.

Ferdinando Bologna, "Gilbert and George," *Il Mattino*, May 13, 1975.

Carter Ratcliff, "The art and artlessness of Gilbert & George," *Arts Magazine*, January 1976, pp. 54–57.

Anthony Haden-Guest, "The Red Sculpture," *Paris Review*, Winter 1976.

Michael Roberts, "The art of living," *Sunday Times*, February 22, 1976.

Lynda Morris, "Gilbert & George," *The Listener*, May 22, 1976.

William Feaver, "'Mental' images," *The Observer*, May 30, 1976.

Shirley Lowe, "Gilbert & George & Us," *Over 21 Magazine*, 1976.

Edward Lucie-Smith, "Ever so nice," *Art & Artists*, March 1977, pp. 27–29.

Jan Zumbrink, "Beeldhouwen met het eigen lichaam," *De Nieuwe Linie*, March 30, 1977.

Dorothy Walker, "Marshmallow Aesthetes," *Hibernia*, February 4, 1977.

Betty van Garrel, "Laat ons hopen dat kunst war is," *Hollands Diep*, March 1977, pp. 46–47.

R. H. Fuchs, "Gilbert & George, Dark Shadow," *Art Monthly*, April 1977.

Mickey Piller, "Wij noemen alles wat we doen skuptuur," *Haagse Post*, April 9, 1977.

Richard Lorber, "Gilbert & George," *ArtForum*, May 1978, pp. 59–60.

Rudy Kousbroek, "De bedrogen verbeelding," *N.R.C. Handelsblad*, March 3, 1978.

Carter Ratcliff, "Down and out with Gilbert & George," *Art in America*, May/June 1978, pp. 92–93.

Lien Heyting, "Wij poetsen elke ochtend onze schoenen," *N.R.C. Handelsblad*, December 7, 1979.

Carter Ratcliff, "Gilbert & George and modern life," *Gilbert and George 1968 to 1980* (exhibition catalogue), Van Abbemuseum, Eindhoven, 1980.

Ted Castle, "Gilbert & George arrive beyond alcohol and sex," *Art Monthly*, November 1980.

Maartin Beks, "Gilbert en George enorm beeldverhaal," *Eindhovens Daglad*, December 6, 1980.

Jan Zumbrink, "Het leven zelf als kunstvorm," *Haarlems Daglad*, December 11, 1980.

Stephen Walker, "Living with Fear and Gilbert and George," *Blitz*, vol. 1, no. 4, 1981.

Simon Wilson, "Modern Fears," *Burlington Magazine*, February 1981.

Mary Blume, "Gilbert and George, From Living Sculpture to Modern Fears," *International Herald Tribune*, January 31–February 1, 1981.

John Roberts, "Gilbert and George at Anthony d'Offay," *Artscribe*, February 1981.

Martin Pouret, "Art and Purity," *ZG*, no. 2, 1981.

Irmeline Lebeer, "Gilbert & George, art for all," *Art Press*, April 1981.

Jean-Hubert Martin, "Gilbert & George, Un entretien avec Jean-Hubert Martin," published by Centre Pompidou, Paris, April 1981.

Mark Francis, "Gilbert and George, An interview with Mark Francis," published by Whitechapel Art Gallery, London, June 1, 1981.

Wim van Mulders, "Gilbert & George: beeldhouwers," *Streven*, July 1981.

Bernard Marcelis, "Gilbert and George: An Itinerary," *Domus*, July 1981.

Waldemar Januszcak, "Making snap judgements," *The Guardian*, July 4, 1981.

Marina Valzey, "Gilbert and George: dandies in despair," *Sunday Times*, July 5, 1981.